The Dissertation Handbook

A Guide to Successful Dissertations

Eileen T. Nickerson
Boston University

Kendall/Hunt
Publishing Company
Dubuque, Iowa

B   403614   01

Contents

List of Figures

Preface

In all my years of dissertation advisement, I have become convinced that there are a number of useful matters that can helpfully be brought to the attention of dissertation authors *both* before and during this process. Despite some individual institutional and faculty preferences on various details, there fortunately is a common core of considerations which can productively be shared with prospective dissertation researchers. As much as possible, this volume is designed to serve as an indispensable resource which makes the process more comprehensible, easier, and hopefully more enjoyable.

It is the intention of the author to review in a simple and straightforward manner a series of dissertation-related matters which often seem bewildering and overwhelming. It is expected that this text will provide a practical "how to do it" guide that will aid and nurture the student at several crucial dissertation phases.

In this text the dissertation process is broken down into little steps or phases in a demystifying, do-able and humane fashion. We begin at the amorphous, stressful beginning stage when one is trying to decide on what, where and how. Then the content of the dissertation proposal is detailed, as well as such aspects as how one goes about choosing and working with a dissertation committee and how one presents and defends the proposal. The final dissertation process of analyzing and writing up the results as well as their implications is discussed. And lastly, the after-dissertation phases of professional presentations and publications are explored.

Biographical Sketches

Hilary E. Bender, Ph.D.

Hilary E. Bender, Ph.D., is a student of the human sciences and human services, having earned two doctorates in them at the University of Pittsburgh and the Catholic University of America and having practiced them in the fields of teaching, psychotherapy and ministry. He has taught at the School of Education of Boston University since 1971. His major interest is in developing a research method particularly appropriate to understanding the human experience.

Steven N. Broder, Ph.D.

Steven N. Broder, Ph.D. is currently Assistant Professor of Psychology and Counseling in the College of Basic Studies at Boston University. Since 1979, he has also been a Clinical Fellow in Psychology, Department of Psychiatry at the Massachusetts General Hospital and Harvard Medical School. Dr. Broder also holds appointments as an Adjunct Assistant Professor at Lesley College and at the School of Education, Boston University Overseas Programs. His publications and research have been in the areas of biofeedback, self-disclosure, adolescent stress, and psychotherapy supervision.

Edward A. Hattauer, Ph.D.

Edward A. Hattauer, Ph.D., is currently Director of the Counseling Center at Potsdam College, State University of New York. Previously, he served as a visiting Assistant Professor for the Boston University Overseas Programs and as Assistant Director of the Center for Life Skills and Human Resource Development of Teachers College, Columbia University where he obtained his Ph.D. Degree in Counseling Psychology. Dr. Hattauer has also been a Peace Corps Volunteer and has extensive experience in consulting, training, and psychosocial program development.

Michael W. Hurst, Ed.D.

Michael W. Hurst, Ed.D. received his S.B. degree from MIT in 1970 and his Ed.M. and Ed.D. degrees from Boston University in 1972 and 1974 respectively. Prior to finishing his doctoral degree, he was an internal statistical consultant and teaching fellow. Subsequent to his graduation, he offered statistical consulting services as an outside consultant to over 100 dissertation students and their committees. He is the author of 23 refereed, published papers; 18 professional presentations; and 7 technical papers. He received a national award for some of his work on stress and mental illness that was conducted as part of a major five year study of air traffic controllers. He currently is Associate Clinical Professor of Psychiatry (Psychology) at Boston University Medical School and is the President of Hurst Associates, Inc., a business psychology consulting firm.

Eileen T. Nickerson, Ph.D.

Eileen T. Nickerson, Ph.D. is a Professor in the Counseling Psychology Program, School of Education, Boston University and also serves as the Co-Director of the Specialization in Counseling Women. She holds a BA degree from the University of Illinois with honors in Sociology, a MA from the University of Minnesota in Educational Psychology and a Ph.D. in Counseling Psychology from Columbia University. She has also studied at Stockholm and Uppsala Universities and has also taught at Harvard University, Northeastern University and the International Graduate School. She has written a dozen texts and some fifty articles, papers and monographs and has directed nearly one hundred dissertation projects in her thirty years of graduate teaching.

Joseph Reimer, Ed.D.

Joseph Reimer, Ed.D., is an Assistant Professor in Boston University's School of Education and Director of the Program in Human Development. He has received an Ed.D. from Harvard University and has also taught at Harvard University, Brandeis University and the Smith College School for Social Work. He is co-author of *Promoting Moral Growth* (Longman) and a number of articles on moral development and education.

Acknowledgments

I would like to thank the faculty, students and administration of the Counseling Psychology Program, School of Education, Boston University and the International Graduate School; as well as colleagues throughout the United States and abroad for their assistance in the formulation of this handbook. I would also like to thank the students who have participated in our Dissertation Colloquia for their thoughtful discussions which have helped to shape this *Dissertation Handbook*.

Specifically, I would also like to thank the contributors (Hilary Bender, Steve Broder, Edward Hattauer, Michael Hurst and Joseph Reimer); and the colleagues who reacted to the chapters (Oliva Espin, Ralph Mosher, Robert Pitcher and Joseph Reimer). Lastly, I need to especially thank my family who patiently endured my endless writing, while supporting me in my endeavors.

Chapter One
The Dissertation Process
Eileen T. Nickerson, Ph.D.

Getting Started

For many persons, the most difficult part of the dissertation process is getting started. It can be a dismaying and painful process for a number of reasons. One may feel pulled in varying directions because of a variety of interests, pressures from faculty and others to follow certain directions, difficulties in narrowing one's focus and the need to develop a reasonable yet doable dissertation project. We have tried to provide the kind of understanding and ideas which will make the dissertation process manageable and possible. A number of guidelines are provided in this text for what initially may seem to be an overwhelming task.

Dissertations are most likely to be successfully completed in reasonable time if one starts to "think dissertation" from the beginning of graduate study. Since graduate school days are hectic ones, many students put this task off to the end of their formal course work. Hopefully, however, you have realized the value of getting an early start and are using this text at an early point in your graduate studies. This gives you an opportunity to explore your interests when doing classroom assignments and projects; as well as to review their research implications in various forums and with your fellow students and professional colleagues.

Whether one begins early or later in their graduate program, the primary task remains to develop a reasonable topic of study from one's scholarly and professional interests. The following section details the choice of a topic emanating from the pursuit and exploration of your professional interests. Your interests of course will be affected and colored by those of your graduate faculty. So in the fullest sense, you will spend time initially articulating your interests as they intersect with those of your faculty and other colleagues. And as you involve yourself regularly in this process, ask yourself these questions: Is this an area or project which merits and needs to be studied further? Does it interest and excite me—would I like to spend time and effort researching this topic?

1

Choosing a Topic

The first and most important aspect of the dissertation process is to select a topic. As a part of this initial assignment it may be well to allow yourself to brainstorm a number of possibilities. It is always easier to eliminate possible topics from your list, than it is to have only one or two possibilities from which to select. Criteria for elimination and selection will be offered later. But in this process it needs to be stressed that candidates often go through three, four and five or more topics before settling on what they will do for their thesis. The process of moving from topic diffusion to topic identity tends to be a lengthy one, in which it is helpful to explore widely, rather than prematurely settling on a topic. At this point, a "shopping list" of possible topic sources is provided below.

Sources for Possible Topics. There are a variety of sources to be tapped in generating your list. These include:

. . . Your professional interests. A question to ask yourself is, what energizes and excites you in your field of study? What aspects do you find personally and professionally meaningful? What area(s) would you like to investigate further? What problems and questions most intrigue you?

. . . The interests and professional areas of inquiry of your faculty and professional colleagues. Mosher (1974) discusses the nature of the process by which we derive research hypotheses from our professional work. Most of your faculty and related personnel (e.g., field site supervisors, etc.) have researchable interests and/or projects which they would be glad to share with you and assist you in the shaping of a topic. Pick their brains!

. . . Dissertations, articles, papers in the area of your interest usually contain a section titled essentially "Further Research"/"Future Research", etc. In these sections the author delineates their sense of "where to from here"—i.e., what future research needs to be done in this area. By reading the manuscript and the author's ideas regarding further research possibilities, you may obtain a sense of the research that has been done in an area, plus future possibilities and needs for further studies.

. . . Populations available for study. The reality of doing a dissertation necessitates having access to the necessary subjects to be studied. At times, you may have to drop an idea for a particular study because there is no available population with which you might conduct it. At other times, you may think about doing a study in a certain area because you know you will be able to obtain the participation of the needed person(s) in your study.

Common Mistakes in Choosing a Topic. Gardner and Beatty (1980, p.8)*
list the following common mistakes in choosing a dissertation topic:

. . . Collecting a lot of information with no particular plan or purpose and
then figuring "I'll make some sense out of this later". If your advisor is
letting you do this, s/he needs help too!

. . . Taking a bunch of data that is already available in your school or work-
place (or a friend's data) and trying to fit some meaningful research
question to it.

. . . Defining your operational terms, objectives, questions, in such an am-
biguous or general way that your deductions, conclusions, etc., are probably invalid or useless.

. . . Not basing research on a theoretical/empirical base. The key to a quality
dissertation is to use a sound theoretical/empirical base for hypothesis
development.

. . . Not making clear your project's assumptions or limitations.

. . . Failure to anticipate rival hypotheses (other possible explanations) for
the outcomes of your study.

Criteria for Selecting a Topic. And Madsen (1983, p. 23) summarizes the
criteria for selecting a topic as:

1. It must sustain your interest and stimulate your imagination.
2. It must be manageable in size.
3. It must be within your range of competence.
4. It must have the potential to make an original contribution to the sum of
human knowledge.

Researching a Topic

Appendices A and D furnish a guide to reference books and periodicals
which you will find at the library. It is also assumed that you have acquired
a working knowledge of your institution's facilities as well as those of the surrounding area. And hopefully, you have remembered that a graduate student's
best friend may well be the reference librarian.

A good starting point of where to look for material on your topic, is to
locate the most recent and relevant articles and/or books on your subject. Then
follow up on their main or major references listed in the text and bibliogra-
phies.

Conduct a computer search on your topic when you have it reasonably
narrowed to some of most of the major parameters of your proposed study.
Computer searches can save considerable time and effort. Such searches may

*From David C. Gardner and Grace J. Beatty. *Dissertation Proposal Guidebook,* 1980. Courtesy
of Charles C. Thomas, Publisher, Springfield, Illinois.

also be cited in your review of the literature to attest to the thoroughness of your search.

Choosing a Committee

Probably no part of the dissertation process is so shrouded in mystifying ambiguity as that of choosing one's dissertation advisor and committee. Yet probably nothing is reputed to be more vital to the success of your mission than the nature and composition of your dissertation committee and your relations and work with them. Conducting and writing up a dissertation study is an emotional as well as an intellectual task; hence some "matchings" of expertise and temperament seem more fortuitous than others.

The process of dissertation chairperson and committee selection varies somewhat at different institutions so you will need to find out what the formal and sometimes informal ground rules are at your university. A university's published program description will contain statements of the formal process followed at your school. Additionally, it makes sense to get to know your available faculty by taking classes with them, reading their publications, attending research seminars which they might offer, etc. The opinion and experience of other students may also be utilized, although there is no substitute for your own judgment and exposure.

Your first task then is to obtain a major advisor or first reader. How does one go about this? Some institutions assign advisors at the beginning of the doctoral education, allowing or encouraging a student to make a different choice for the dissertation advisor if it is deemed desirable for a variety of reasons, most usually because of expertise and interest in the student's proposed topic. Other programs assign one faculty member as the initial advisor until a dissertation sponsor is appointed or selected.

If a choice of advisors is allowed, how does one go about making that vital choice? The aim and objective of the process of obtaining the first reader or principal dissertation advisor should be to find a faculty member with whom one can work comfortably, yet one who is interested in and possesses expertise in the area which you are selecting for investigation. Other qualities that are frequently listed as important are that the first reader be sympathetic yet demanding, helpful in bringing forth your best efforts and that she or he be someone who is respected by their colleagues. As noted previously, exposure to and experience with your faculty will probably be your best guide in these deliberations.

And what about the rest of the committee? At some institutions, the remainder of the committee is assigned by the department or division director. Other institutions allow the student to "invite" the other committee members to join the committee. In the later instance, it is usually expected that the student will check with the major reader who probably has some useful suggestions, as well as being receptive to yours. From such a conference, often

4

comes a prioritized list from which the student may proceed to complete this committee selection process.

Gardner and Beatty (1980) indicate that while working closely with your advisor in selecting the committee, you should "insist on your right as a 'consumer' to have input into the selection of your doctoral committee" (p. 81). They also strongly advocate selecting highly successful and qualified people claiming they rarely have "insecure egos which need to be fed by putting others down. The 'tougher' your committee (meaning the more qualified), the 'easier' it will be" (p. 81).

One of my colleagues also advises that one of their committee selections be a statistician or someone particularly versed in your research methodology. However, it may not make sense to have someone on the committee who has little experience and interest in your subject. Furthermore, most universities allow you to have consultants and you may secure some highly specific expertise in this manner. Chapter Six discusses in more detail the possible use of a consultant.

That usual procedure after you and your first dissertation reader have developed an appropriate list of candidates for committee membership, is to request a meeting with them to discuss your dissertation, accompanying the request with a copy of a brief prospectus of your proposed study. If they express interest and availability, a verbal invitation to become a committee member could then be appropriately proferred. In some instances, your advisor may do this task for you. In any event, you are another step on the way when this aspect of the process seems to be in place.

Some advisors recommend having at least one committee member more than the requisite minimum number. Then if one committee member resigns from the committee, the university or life itself, you do not have to frantically scramble for a last minute replacement. Given the relative instability of our times, it may be an idea worth considering. However, every added committee member, limits your degrees of freedom when it comes to scheduling of dissertation hearings, etc.

Working with the Committee

After you have chosen your topic, done the necessary library research and selected your committee, you will address yourself to formulating the proposal and working with your committee on your proposal, the data analysis and the final dissertation draft. Chapter Two details what is contained in the proposal and the proposal approval process. Chapter Three will discuss various stylistic considerations in preparing the dissertation manuscript. Chapter Eight will delineate what is contained in the final chapters of the dissertation, as well as reviewing with you what is involved in the final dissertation approval process. Several aspects of appropriate and effective committee workings and procedures however, need to be considered here at the outset, as it is again in Chapter Seven.

Role of the Advisor. As noted earlier in the section about the selection of committee members, your major dissertation advisor or first reader is a crucial link in developing your study and working constructively with your committee. Ideally this person is a valued mentor, who enjoys your trust. Most aspects and details of the process will first be shared with this person.

This sharing process includes the initial ideas you have for a dissertation study, a detailed outline and the initial prospectus of the study. You and your first reader will agree upon when and how this data will be shared in turn with the other committee members. As indicated, a prospectus of the prepared study, Figure 1, and a discussion of it usually preceeds a direct invitation to join the committee.

Figure 1
Proposed Dissertation Project

Your Name, Address
A. Proposed Topic
B. One-two paragraph prospectus of proposed topic
C. References
D. Where and how you may be reached

Submission of the Proposal*

As you write chapters of the proposal, you usually first submit them to your first reader; and then after revisions, to the other members of the committee; although your advisor may suggest that they be simultaneously submitted to all members. For the most part, if a committee member does agree to read your rough draft s/he is doing you a favor because it is the primary responsibility of the chairperson to get the draft in shape so that the committee will approve it. If you have any doubts on this, check with your first reader and then your committee members to see how they feel and what their working preferences are.

When you turn dissertation copy into your advisor, give her/him an outline of the proposal or total thesis and at least one chapter. S/he will read them carefully and indicate her/his reactions. Therefore, be sure that you leave wide margins and that you have double spaced everything. It probably goes without saying that this should be a typed copy. After your advisor has re-

*Adapted in part from Fahrquhar, W. W. (1968). *Directions for Theses Preparation;* and Nickerson, E. T. and Robertson, L. W. (1978). *A Dissertation Preparation Handbook;* Unpublished Manuscript, Michigan State and Boston Universities, respectively.

sponded to the first chapter, and after you have incorporated any modifications suggested by her/him, you may proceed to the remaining chapters. You are not expected to retype the rough draft (until the last draft), unless it is too messy. Make sure that when you hand the copy back to your advisor, s/he can read easily what it is that you have corrected. You may use inserts, pinned-on or stapled sheets, and whatever else your ingenuity will allow. Remember, a rough draft is not an exercise in perfectionism, so use the most expedient way to clearly show how you have altered your copy.

Problems with Committee Members. Hopefully all your committee members are colleagues who hold each other in reasonable esteem. If, however, seemingly insoluble conflicts arise, discuss the situation with your advisor, as elaborated upon in Chapters Two and Seven. It is possible to remove a member of the Committee at the pre-proposal stage, if that is really desired by you. Check with your first reader regarding such procedures. However, it is always best to try to work things out. If they cannot be, it is also appropriate to be responsibly assertive about your rights. After all, it is your professional future which is of prime concern. If you have more than the requisite minimum number of faculty members, the deletion of a committee member merely means having one less committee member. If you have only the minimum number and one drops out or is dropped, you will have to go looking again and perhaps under somewhat more awkward and/or pressured circumstances.

Overview of the Text

The successful completion of a dissertation and the process itself is detailed in the chapters to follow. The drafting, contents and approval of a proposal is delineated in the next chapter (Chapter Two). In Chapter Three all the fascinating details involved in stylistic dissertation considerations, such as captions, margins, etc., are delineated. In Chapters Four and Five considerations involved in Experimental and Qualitative types of research design are explored. In Chapter Six concerns regarding the use of a statistical consultant are shared; and in Chapter Seven concerns about developmental difficulties in dissertating are similarly examined. Chapter Eight involves developing the last chapters in the dissertations, which are written after the data collection and analysis phases. And the last of the chapters, Chapter Nine, is addressed to that glorious phase, life after the dissertation. Hopefully, all the queries and doubts you will ever have about the process will be addressed for you. It is expected that this text will provide a suitable guide on the journey you are about to take.

Chapter Two
Formulating and Writing the Proposal
Eileen T. Nickerson, Ph.D.

When to Start Writing

One of the frequent questions dissertation advisees ask is how to determine when one has read, thought and talked about their topic enough to write the proposal. The questions sounds simple and is usually answered in a more arbitrary fashion than reality dictates.

Ideally you begin to write when you have read everything important and pertinent to your topic and you have discussed at length your ideas with members of your committee and perhaps, with members of a research seminar group. You also have developed an outline of what you need to cover—i.e., the various parts that constitute a proposal. You've sharpened your pencils, compiled a neat stack of reference cards, filled your coffee cup, put out the cat/dog and cleared your work space. Then indeed you are ready!

Before you actually start writing, it would be helpful to organize your notes into the three chapters that will constitute your proposal (Figure 2). While it is possible to still cover the topics as indicated without organizing them into chapters, doing so can make the final writing process easier. It may also be useful to work on different parts of the three chapters according to one's personal preference and then cut and paste them into an orderly sequence. That is, you may feel moved to write up one of the instruments one morning, work on the limitations section on another and move back to the definitions part at another time.

One aspect that is imperative though is to develop an adequate 'Statement of the Problem' at an early stage. In a sense, the 'Statement of the Problem' is the organizational theme of your dissertation. It will be reflected in and consonant with all other parts of your dissertation (e.g., the title, the review of the literature, the hypotheses or major research questions, etc.).

How to Write the Proposal*

Contemplating the writing of a dissertation proposal can have an overwhelming effect. If you consider the task of writing the entire proposal all at

---

*Adapted in part from Fahrquhar, W. W. (1968), *Directions for Theses Preparation;* and Nickerson, E. T. and Robertson, L. W. (1978), *A Dissertation Preparation Handbook;* Unpublished manuscripts, Michigan State and Boston Universities, respectively.

Figure 2
Suggested Outline for a Research Proposal

The outline format must remain flexible and consistent with the purpose and structure of each study. The one appearing below is meant to suggest the contents of each of the major sections of the paper. A deviation from this, following the framework suggested by a related research article, is very much in order. The outline, however, should be clearly set up in a logical, readable form.

Title

Make the title specific, concise, instructive and distinctive.

I. *Introduction and Statement of the Problem*

Background of the problem
Major questions and objectives of the study
Significance and rationale of the problem in its broader aspects
Operational definitions of "key" concepts
Hypotheses to be tested or major research questions
Summary and brief overview of the chapters to follow

II. *Review of Related Research*

Review briefly, critically and clearly research related to your study and make its relationship to your proposed study explicit.

II. *Procedures*

State clearly the methods to be used in gathering data to answer the questions or to test the hypotheses involved. For example:

a. Indicate the techniques to be employed (interview, questionnaire, tests, drawings, observations, analysis of published evidence, etc.).
b. Indicate the kinds of subjects or sources (persons or groups, journals, case studies, original documents, textbooks, etc.) to which the techniques will be applied.
c. Enumerate the specific data to be obtained from the method described.
d. Delineate your research design and the hypotheses or major research questions to be addressed.
e. Present appropriate methods of handling the data.
f. Indicate the limitations involved in your study.
g. Briefly outline the expected results.

once, you will probably be "immobilized". Instead, consider approaching the task by deciding to write parts of chapters that will dovetail together. If you first develop an outline (Figure 2), set intermediate goals for yourself around the production of a single part of the outline at a time, you will find that the task readily begins to fall into place. In fact, it might help you to start if you expand or adopt the dissertation outline you develop into a table of contents, realizing that as you progress you will put your own stamp of creativity and originality onto the skeletal outline.

Over the years the format of a thesis has become somewhat standardized. Therefore, it is not necessary for you to start from scratch in preparing your overall outline. Each chapter has its usual content and if you will examine the following sections carefully (as well as Chapters Three and Eight), you will find a way to organize your proposal (see Figure 2). It should be stressed that this suggested outline is intended to be a flexible one, subject to alterations as the dissertation develops.

The point of writing in smaller units needs to be looked at a little more carefully. Generally, it is much more efficient to write a complete section— such as a chapter—and then go back and revise the rough spots. The experience of seasoned writers has been that writing progresses most efficiently when they write a section, let it "set" for two or three days, edit it carefully, looking for particular weaknesses, and then let it "set" for two or three days again. At the end of this time the section may be ready to show to some colleague or editor for her/his critical eye.

A number of important stylistic considerations to guide your writing will be reviewed in the chapter (three) which follows. You would be wise to re-review this chapter when you are about to do your final dissertation writing. However, here are some additional suggestions which may help you at both the proposal and final writing stage.

. . . Develop a set of manila folders, one for each chapter;
. . . List on each folder the types of information or topics which need to be included in the chapter;
. . . As you write up a section file it in the appropriate folder;
. . . When you have written a series of sections, try putting them together in a larger section;
. . . While writing in parts, keep your dissertation and chapter content outline handy so that you can keep the overall picture of 'gestalt' clearly in mind as you formulate parts of the project;
. . . As you eliminate "good research ideas" (e.g., methodology, instrumentation, populations, etc.,) which are promising but not appropriate for your project, note these and file under "Future Research Directions" for your final chapter. You will find that these ITEMS will be a helpful reminder of what still needs doing at a time when you are weary and feeling creatively pressed;

. . . When reviewing the literature, collect quotes and anecdotal material which may help you illustrate, reinforce or support your expected findings;

. . . Use captions through the chapters to aid your reader to follow your cognitive map or overall organizational scheme.

The Proposal Itself

The following sections will be organized along the lines of the proposal and final dissertation project—that is, they will constitute the first three chapters of your thesis. Very simply stated, Chapter I will essentially cover the *"what"* aspects of your project; Chapter II will cover what others have studied and written on the subject; and Chapter III details the *"how"* of your project, that is, how it will be carried out.

Proposal: Chapter One — The Problem

Chapter One usually consists of the following sections in the order shown:

Background of the Problem
Rationale and Significance of the Problem
Statement of the Problem
General Hypotheses or Major Research Questions
Definitions
Summary and Overview

Background of the Problem. This section typically introduces your reader to your project by reviewing its history and status—that is, what led you to this particular problem and your orientation to it. This is one part where your personal saga on the way to evolving your project may be revealed. It should be to the point, however, and not overly sentimental nor personal, but as compelling as your scholarly language will allow it to be.

Rationale and Significance of the Problem. This section is a further articulation of the *"why"* of your problem, particularly in terms of its relevance and value to the field your study covers. It should be a clear exposition of the merits of your study, its place in the field, what it might contribute to theory, practice and scholarship. When well presented, it lays to rest your readers concerns, and hopefully yours, as to why you are bothering with this project, why it needs to be done, and what its significance will be.

While modesty and an impersonal tone are considered to be hallmarks of scientific writing, it is important within the confines of scholarly formulation to give us a sense of the excitement, the richness of your problem and your perceptions of these dimensions. It is also helpful to keep this sense of mission in focus throughout, ending your dissertation on the zestful note with which you initially framed your journey.

11

Statement of the Problem. By the time you have finished the preceding sections, you should have your reader well primed for this section—your clear statement of what you will be doing in your study. This section should be relatively brief, direct and explicit. At an appropriate point, you will write "It is the purpose of this study to"; so that your reader, no matter how unsophisticated, will have exact understanding of what your project will undertake to do.

General Hypotheses / Major Research Questions. Following the Statement of the Problem you will detail more precisely what either your General Hypotheses or Major Research Questions are; depending, generally speaking, upon whether yours is a quantitative or qualitative type of study. You may note at this point in the text, that the hypotheses will be restated in testable form in the third chapter. Some examples of broadly stated general hypotheses might be:

It is hypothesized that . . .

. . . a positive relationship exists between the self esteem of sixth graders and their level of reading achievement.

. . . the androgyny level of young adult men and women is positively related to their perceived need for both autonomy and intimacy.

Definitions. Usually the General Hypotheses or Major Research Questions section is followed by an operational definition of all the major concepts and terms to be employed in your study. Such definitions might include concepts employed in the preceding examples such as self esteem, reading achievement, androgyny, autonomy and intimacy. It should cover all the essential terms in your Statement of the Problem.

One might start this section by giving the general dictionary and specific professional definitions of the terms, followed by an operational delineation of the term. That is, a clear statement of how the terms will be employed in your (i.e., "this") study. In a sense these definitions help your reader follow you throughout your text.

Summary and Overview (of Chapter One). Each chapter will conclude with a brief and well integrated overview of what you have covered. Chapter One is no exception. Additionally, Chapter One should end with a clear and concise overview of what the following chapters will contain. No mysteries here. For proposal purposes, merely preview Chapter Two and Three. For the final dissertation, review the contents of all the chapters to follow, thereby clearly setting the stage for what is to come.

Proposal: Chapter Two — Review of the Literature

Introduction to the Review of the Literature. Again in our usual clear and scholarly fashion, we begin the review with one or two paragraphs which organize the chapter for the reader, providing the reader a "cognitive map" of the chapter's direction. We say such exciting things as . . . in the first part of this review . . . and secondly . . . etc., etc. Incidentally, you actually need to follow the organizational format you delineate, signaling this schema by the use of your, by now familiar, organizing tool, the caption. And everything which you indicate will be covered in the chapter should be there in the order presented and nothing else.

What to Review and How! * The review of the literature may be particularly difficult because you may have problems briefly summarizing the common shortcomings of previous research which supports the rationale for your study. The more extensive the previous work, the more difficult the preparation of this chapter becomes. Nonetheless, this rationale needs to be clearly stated in the beginning and ending of your review.

You may also find that there are several complete bodies of literature that relate to what you are doing. You face the question then of which of these you review in depth or whether it is necessary for you to review all of them. Generally, the solution is worked out as follows. One, you review in depth those studies which are almost identical to yours, indicating their strengths and weaknesses and how their findings might be incorporated or improved upon in your research design. Two, those studies which have a bearing on your problem but are not directly related to it, can be put into a general review of several paragraphs or pages to bring the reader closer to your particular problem. In this case, you may cite summaries that others have pulled together on the topic. It is highly unlikely that any area of "investigatory saturation" has not somewhere along the line been reviewed in either a professional journal or a doctoral thesis. Remember, however, that you are responsible for the authenticity of the summary, so you should read the original accounts of investigations that are particularly germane to your study. In writing your summary, the most straightforward presentation is to proceed from the general idea of relevant research to those which are more specific to the particular research issues of your dissertation.

However, if you have chosen a topic on which there has been little previous research, do not panic. It is acceptable for you to review the two or three more closely allied studies that are the extent of the literature in your area of research.

---

*Adapted in part from Farquhar, W. W. (1968), *Directions for Theses Preparation;* and Nickerson, E. T. and Robertson, L. W. (1978). *A Dissertation Preparation Handbook;* Unpublished Manuscripts, Michigan State and Boston Universities, respectively.

Remember that you will always need to also critically review the literature pertaining to the major theoretical construct(s) of your study. It is necessary to integrate and synthesize these conceptualizations, including those which will form the theoretical framework of your study.

Summary (of the Review of the Literature). Too often the review of the literature appears as an interruption to fill an apparent vacuum between Chapters One and Three. In reality, this chapter will help solidly build the case for the rationale and significance of your study, including its place and status in the field of study you are covering. It is particularly desirable in this process to include a discussion section at the end of the review, in which the implications of the previous studies are pulled together and the direction to be taken in the third chapter pointed out. You will show how you intend to use what you have found in your review of the literature in your study, which will be detailed (and it will!) in the chapter which follows.

Proposal: Chapter Three—Procedures

Chapter Three contains your "plan of operation"—i.e., your detailed account of how your study is to be carried out. Depending on the nature of your research procedures (e.g., experimental, quasi-experimental or qualitative, etc.), Chapter Three usually consists of the following sections:

Introduction (or Overview of the Chapter)
Sample/Population To Be Studied
Instrumentation
Intervention (if one is to be employed)
Data Collection Procedures
Research Design
Research Hypotheses or Major Research Questions
Treatment of the Data
Limitations
Summary

Sample Studied. You should specify the nature of your sample, indicating the population from which it came. In the sample specification you should give the anticipated sex, age range, geographical location and all other vital demographic data you can accumulate on your particular group. In the final dissertation the actual characteristics of your sample will also be provided in the text and in the accompanying tables. This is important because future researchers may want to replicate your study (when you become famous for your discoveries of course!!).

While you may wish to become famous, the community and people you studied may not, so we disguise the identities of our sample. For example, rather than indicating that we studied students attending Newton North High

School, we might describe them as students attending a large high school (indicate approximate yearly student census) in an urban center in the northeastern part of the United States.

In the section titled Data Collection Procedures, you will indicate whether the persons studied were requested to give informed consent and if so, the actual *Letter of Informed Consent* will be provided in the Appendix (See Appendix C). There are some selected instances when we do not ask for informed consent—for example, when we are using already existing group test data from which no individual's status can be discerned. Otherwise, we must request participation permission from those we study; or if minors, from their parents or guardians. The American Psychological Association (1982) has published a helpful monograph titled *"Ethical Principles in the Conduct of Research With Human Participants;"* and the December 1981 issue of *Academe* (*67*, 6, 358–370) provides a comprehensive review of federal regulations governing research on human subjects. These regulations may be periodically updated.

Our usual concerns in evolving *Informed Consent* are the following:

. . . to give our subjects a general sense of our study without 'giving away' our hypotheses (i.e., "In this study, I will be attempting to study origins of self esteem.");

. . . to assure subjects studied that their responses will be confidential and in no way, will they be able to be identified through them;

. . . their participation or non-participation in the study will not affect them adversely (e.g., their grades in a course, their likelihood of being seen for treatment, etc.);

. . . that they may discontinue their participation at any point without adverse effect.

Additionally, a section should be provided at the bottom of the letter in which they can indicate by providing their name and address (on the bottom section, to be spearated from the letter) if they wish to be provided with a summary of the general results. Generally, a copy of the Abstract will suffice for this purpose, though you may wish to visit the group studied and provide them with a verbal account of your findings as well. The general ethical principle is that people who give of themselves in our studies deserve feedback. Hopefully, the end product of our work will benefit and enlighten others; as well as the persons studied.

Instrumentation. In this section each vehicle you have used to collect data (e.g., test measure, interview, participant observation, survey, etc.) will be detailed. Typically, the information needed includes: Name of Instrument, Acronym, and Reference(s); Nature, Content and Disposition of the Instrument; Reliability and Validity Data Regarding the Instrument (if any), with a copy of the instrument provided in the Appendix (and referred to in the text). If you have developed a new instrument and you think it constitutes a particular contribution, you may even wish to write a separate chapter or section on it. At any rate, details of the development and use, thus far, will be essential.

After providing identifying information regarding an instrument (e.g, full description, acronym and references), you will first describe your instrument in terms of what it is and what it purports to measure and how it was developed. In this process you will succinctly summarize all the research pertaining to this instrument, including normative data relevant to your study.

Secondly, reliability data, if any, pertaining to the instrument being reviewed, should be provided. You would do well to also include your reliability estimates for your particular sample of investigation. Many of you express an inclination to move these findings into a later chapter on analysis of results. This is an inappropriate move because when you calculate the reliability for the particular group you studied you are merely trying to establish more firmly your independent variable; therefore, what you find cannot in all honesty be classified as a result. The fact that it is necessary for you to establish the reliability of your instruments cannot be emphasized too much!

You will also need to review the validity, as well as the reliability data, for *each* of your instruments. Include in your review of the validity evidence notations as to the nature and extent of the validity evidence (e.g., only minimal concurrent validity and seeming construct validity). It is essential that you take a stand as to the confidence in the reliability and validity one may ascribe to the instruments you use in your study. You are not to be faulted for using an instrument with little established reliability and validity—only for failing to note and to take it into account.

There are some special considerations which apply to the reporting of the instrument employed in qualitative methodological studies and these are aptly discussed in the chapter on Qualitative Research, to which the reader is referred.

Intervention(s). If your study employs an intervention, whether it is for example, an educational, curricular or therapeutic one; the proposed nature of that intervention needs to be provided in this section, with a completely documented review of its content being provided in the Appendices and referred to in the text. Thus, any practitioner or researcher wishing to use your intervention, should be able to replicate it exactly from the description you provide.

Data Collection Procedures. This section will be of immeasurable benefit to you in the conduct and interpretation of your study, for it will detail precisely the steps to be followed in the collection of your data. Its your chance to leave no stone unturned in thinking through and planning for all the aspects necessarily involved in your study.

In the eventuality that a proposed data collection procedure cannot actually be followed during the study (it does happen), do not give up in despair or try to hide the deviation. The desired response to this happening is to circulate a memorandum to the committee, indicating what has transpired and your proposed resolution. Accompany it with a request they they notify you within 2 (or 3) weeks, if there are any questions, etc. And of course, provide them with information as to where they might reach you. One of the most valuable parts of your dissertation account, will be the discussion of the problems and issues which arose in trying to carry out your study. Future students cannot learn from previous researchers without candid presentations of their inquiries such as the one you will provide.

Research Design. Include here a statement as to the type of research design you have employed in the study (a la Campbell and Stanley, 1963), or some other acceptable text on research design accompanied with a diagram of the design and an account of its positive virtues and its limitations vis-a-vis your study. There are a number of reputable texts on various types of research design (experimental, quasi-experimental and qualitative) to which you are referred (see References); as well as other sections of this text referring to research design. (See chapters four and five).

Research Hypotheses or Major Research Questions. In the third chapter you typically restate your statistical or testable hypotheses or major research questions. If you have directional hypotheses these are also stated. In other words, you will note your hypotheses and their directional alternatives, and how they will be measured (with your instruments). Many authors find it helpful to translate the hypothesis from word statements to symbols. In the illustration below you will see both.

> Research Hypothesis: No difference will be found in empathy as measured by average test performance on the Big Name Test of Empathy between counseled and non-counseled groups.

Symbolically:	Ho: $M_1 = M_2$
Legend:	M_1 = Counseled group mean: M_2 = Non-counseled

If your study employs research questions rather than testable hypotheses, the finite articulation of such questions is further addressed in the Chapter on Qualitative Research Design.

Treatment of the Data. In the third chapter you also need to designate which statistical formats you will use to test your hypotheses and/or the manner in which you will handle your data. It helps if you include a discussion of the appropriateness of the models and their associated assumptions. If you make certain assumptions about the nature of your data, such as normality or homogeneity, you should give the readers some cues to help them understand why you think they are warranted. Remember, too, that you should use the most

17

powerful model appropriate for your data. You need not state commonly acceptable statistical formulas nor do you need to derive them for the reader's benefit. However, if by chance you should use a statistical formula or mode of handling which is not generally accessible to the reader, you should state it with full interpretation of all the principles and symbols, and with the necessary references.

Limitations. Review here all the limitations of your dissertation—including those pertaining to the sample, instruments, design, etc. Your objective here is, of course, to acknowledge those factors which will limit the generalizability of your results. This section will prove helpful in terms of eventually explaining your results. Your limitations carefully and non-defensively articulated will hence ultimately serve you well. A limitation is after all, just that, a limitation; and *all* studies have their share of them. Your task is to indicate and take into account those which will affect your results.

Summmary (of Chapter Three). As noted in previous sections, your summary sections are important opportunities for you to tie a chapter together by succinctly providing the highlights. You need to remember that if your readers will read anything, they will read your summary (cheerful thought). And how does one write a useful summary?—by writing and rewriting and rewriting. Its as magical as that.

The Problem Hearing/Proposal Approval

Mystery and rumor abound when it comes to the Problem Hearing/Proposal Approval stage. While there may be some vicarious pleasure to be obtained from spreading or being the recipient of "scary stories" regarding this phase, there may be more to be gained from a more objective and rational sense of this process.

When Are You Ready for Proposal Approval? Academic faculties vary somewhat in the exact nature of the process to be followed, but generally speaking, you are ready for the problem hearing and/or proposal approval when your dissertation chairperson gives you the nod and says you are ready to have a problem hearing and/or proposal approval. Practically speaking, this means that all parts of the proposal have been thought about and written out in the form of a Proposal document, which is circulated to all the committee members *minimally* one week before the problem hearing and/or approval is requested.

In some institutional settings, this "go ahead signal" means contacting your committee members for a time when all can get together and discuss your proposal (i.e., a problem hearing). This often proves to be one of the most maddening parts of the process since you and your committee members are all busy people with little spare time in common.

Probably it is around such matters as deciding when one is ready for a problem hearing or the proposal to be approved, finding time with a busy group of people and meeting institutional deadlines, that the greatest number of personal issues get played out. Some students react by becoming demanding—insisting that calls be instantly returned, that the committee member agrees to inconvenient morning time periods (e.g., early morning, late evening or weekend hours), to overnight reading deadlines, etc. Others may become sullen, withdrawn and withholding. And still others may attempt to play one committee member against another by reports of cooperation, approval, etc., from others to the member seen as less helpful, etc. This is precisely the time when you and your advisor need to call upon previously established trust levels and "hash out" the problems you are encountering and a facilitative approach to them. A problem solving approach and perhaps some counseling sessions are often in order. Crises can be seized as opportunities to fuller personal and professional development in a number of ways.

The Approval Process. Whether it is merely a matter of circulating your completed proposal under your Advisor's direction for the signed approval of your committee members, or holding a meeting (i.e., the Problem Hearing) to discuss and then approve your proposed project; the purpose of this endeavor is to make sure that you are getting the benefit of your committee's possible contributions for the improvement of your project, believe it or not! That is, it is everyone's (yours and the committee members) 'last chance' to think singly and collectively about your project and give you the benefit of their experience and ideas *before* you begin. I often say to students that this process can be an exciting intellectual experience for all concerned (an easier thing for an advisor to say than a student?).

The Problem Hearing. If the proposal is to be "passed upon" during a committee meeting, your advisor will often:

. . . ask you to initially orally present your proposed dissertation project which may include a slide presentation of the design of the study, etc.;

. . . then ask the committee members to comment on your proposal after your presentation;

. . . take notes of the comments for your future reference, so that your energies will be freed for attending to the comments, etc.;

. . . solicit the consensus of the committee as to any proposed changes in your proposed project (usually asking you to leave the premises while this discussion is taking place);

. . . reconvene the meeting to convey to you the sense of the committee's recommendations;

. . . congratulate you for your progress to date and wish you well in carrying out your proposed study (hooray!)!

Possible Program Hearing Queries. While varying questions may be asked about your proposed dissertation project, many of them directed at clarifying specific aspects of your proposal, following are the type of general queries which might legitimately be asked at a problem hearing. They all pertain to various parts of the proposed project to which you have already given thought and will hopefully address in your written proposal and problem hearing presentation. They are presented here as reminders of areas which you might usefully briefly review with your committee at the beginning of the problem hearing. The questions include:

. . . Why this study? What is its value and worth? What have others done on the subject?

. . . Why this sample of persons for your study? Are they the most appropriate persons to be studied in this manner?

. . . Why this particular treatment? What is the basis for choosing, designing it? Can it be used by others in a similar situation?

. . . Why this instrument? Is it the best available for your purposes? What is its reliability, validity data?

. . . Why this methodology? This research design? Does it fit your problem? Is there a better approach? A better research design?

. . . Why this particular treatment of the data? Is the procedure you have chosen for data analysis the wisest? Does it fit the data you have? Will your treatment of the data allow you to ask the questions you want to answer?

. . . What do you think you will know/learn after the study that you don't know now?

Then, after the desired time for celebrating this "marker" event—i.e., the approval of your proposed study—you will begin the data collection phase. To aid you in this process the following sections are designed to help you in the successive phases—data collection and final write-up; as well as examining more comprehensively stylistic and research design considerations. Take pride in the distance you've come, recognize that you are well on your way to the successful completion of your dissertation, and keep going!

Chapter Three
Organizational and Stylistic Considerations

Eileen T. Nickerson, Ph.D.

Introduction

An assumption is made here that you have read the prior two chapters on the dissertation process (Chapter One) and the proposal itself (Chapter Two). Safe assumption or not, it should prove helpful to read this chapter interchangeably with the previous chapters and with Chapters Seven and Eight which deals with the write-up of your results and their implications. For in this chapter we will deal with your favorite organizational and stylistic considerations involved in writing a dissertation—these include, for example, the usual order of presentation, introductions, summaries, preparing the abstract, titling your dissertation, and preparing the manuscript.

Organizational Considerations

The Usual Order of Presentation

The usual order of presentation of the contents of your dissertation is as shown in Figure 3 below and discussed in the pages which follow. However, before proceeding, the usual injunction to *also* refer to any guidelines which your specific institution requires is useful advice to follow.

Preliminaries (Front Matter). The preliminaries, or front matter, of a dissertation typically consists of any or all of the following (as noted in Figure 3): Title Page, Copyright, Approval Page, Acknowledgements, Abstract, Table of Contents, Lists of Tables, Figures.

Titling the Dissertation. Since you have comprehensively surveyed the literature in your chosen field of study, you are well aware of the importance of papers and books on a subject. A dissertation study for example, may be a valuable resource for other scholars but, only if it can be easily located. Modern reference retrieval systems use the words in the title to locate a dissertation. Hence, you will need to pay careful attention to a brief yet fully informing title for your study (See Figure 4).

Compounding the importance of this 'titling process' is the contemporary trend toward shorter, more inclusive titles and scholarly dissemination requirements. The task is to provide a short, meaningful description of the con-

Figure 3
The Usual Order of Dissertation Content

1. Title Page
2. Copyright Notice (if applicable) as follows:
   Copyright by
   ELIZABETH JAYNE STEWART (full legal name)
   1986 (date of publication)
3. Readers' Approval Page
4. Acknowledgements
5. Abstract
6. Preface (optional)
7. Table of Contents
8. List of Figures and Tables (if any)
9. List of Illustrations (if any)
10. Introduction (if any)
11. Text (Chapters One through Five, or more)
12. Appendices (if any)
13. Bibliography
14. Vita (if required)

tents of your study, in which you avoid oblique references. Also, use word substitutes for formulas, symbols and acronyms.

Copyright Page. Since the microfilming of a dissertation is a form of publication, you need to follow all laws regarding copyrighting. As noted later in the chapter, University Microfilms publishes a helpful pamphlet titled, Preparing Your Dissertation for Microfilming, available through your library. Figure 5 illustrates a sample copyright notice.

Readers Approval Page. Most institutions have a specific format for the purpose of obtaining the signed approval of the dissertation committee. Some universities include other signatures such as the graduate dean and some incorporate these signatures with the title page. A sample approval sheet format is provided in Figure 6, although usually it occupies a full page. It is important to accurately list the members of the committee and their academic rank.

Acknowledgements. This section provides an opportunity to express appreciation to your dissertation committee, colleagues and participants who have been helpful to you in this process. Some include supportive family members, as well as those who have provided clerical, statistical and/or technical assistance.

22

Figure 4
Sample Format for the Title Page

UNIVERSITY

NAME OF SCHOOL

DISSERTATION OR THESIS

TITLE IN FULL CAPITALS

by

Name of Student in Full

Previous Degrees, Colleges, Date

submitted in partial fulfillment

of the

requirements for the degree of

_____

DATE (MONTH, YEAR)

Figure 5
Sample Copyright Page

Figure 6
Sample Format for Readers' Approval Sheet

Approved by

First Reader

               Academic Rank _____

Second Reader

               Academic Rank _____

Third Reader

               Academic Rank _____

Abstract. As noted in the later part of this chapter, universities require that a doctoral candidate submit an abstract (a brief descriptive summary) of the dissertation. The abstract is usually placed before the Table of Contents and after the Acknowledgements section. The graduate office sends a copy of the abstract to University Microfilms, which prints an abstract in *Dissertation Abstracts International* (DAI) for each dissertation available on microfilm. Abstracts published in DAI are limited to a maximum of three hundred and fifty words.

The abstract should include a statement of the problem or issue, a brief description of the research method and design, major findings and their significance, and the conclusions. (See the sample abstract form contained in Figure 7).

Table of Contents. Although the table of contents in a book usually follows the preface and acknowledgments, the accepted practice for a thesis or dissertation is to place the table of contents before the text. The table of contents should list all elements of the preliminaries, the chapter (part or section) titles, the main headings, and subheadings, the reference materials and appendices. The beginning page number for each section is indicated along the right-hand

---

TITLE OF DISSERTATION IN FULL CAPITALS

(Order No.   )*

NAME IN FULL, DEGREE

UNIVERSITY / SCHOOL, DATE

Major Professor: NAME IN FULL, RANK

(All abstracts are limited to 350 words. Consult the Agreement
form of University Microfilms for this requirement.)

(TEXT OF ABSTRACT)

---

*The Order # is assigned by University Microfilms but the notation appears here.

margin. The numbering of chapters and the wording, capitalization and punctuation (if any) of titles and headings should be exactly the same as they are
in the text.

Lists of Tables, Figures and Illustrations. Lists of tables, figures, and/or
plates should follow the table of contents. Each of these types of illustrative
matter should be listed together on a separate page. Charts, graphs, maps,
and illustrations of other kinds are usually grouped as figures, but they may
be designated by their more descriptive names, as in "Chart 3" or "Map 7."
Full-page illustrations, including photographs, are usually called plates and
are listed after the list of figures. When there are only two or three tables or
figures in a thesis or dissertation, local policy may permit omission of a listing
in the front matter. All captions should appear in the listing exactly as they
are in the text.

The Text (or Main Body)

Introductions to Chapters: A Cognitive Map. Since we are not writing a mystery novel (later perhaps?), it is helpful to begin each chapter with an introductory section in which you provide your reader with a basic overall outline of the contents of the chapter. This cognitive map of the chapter may begin with the simple but clear expository statement: "In this chapter, the following topics will be covered. . . ." Whatever you promise to cover however, deliver on those expectations and in the order indicated.

In Chapters Two (The Dissertation Process) and Eight (The Final Dissertation), the typical content found in a chapter and useful indicators of topics to be covered in an introductory paragraph are addressed. The main point of an *Introduction* to a chapter is to provide your reader a clear cognitive sense of what is to be found in the chapter. No mysteries are contained in dissertation writing—the plot is clearly and definitively shared!

Captions: Following a Cognitive Map. It is not clear to me why, but many dissertation writers seem to be adverse to using captions—a useful guide to your cognitive map. Ideally, all the topical sections outlined in your introductory paragraph will be marked by captions in the paragraphs which follow. Thus, your reader is given a clear guide to the chapters contents in the introductory paragraph(s), with captions 'lighting the way' as your reader progresses. And note that the headings (captions) you use should not be presented in Roman numerals or all capital letters.

Captions: Figures, Graphs and Tables. If you are using the American Psychological Association's (APA) *Publication Manual* (1983), the Turabian Format (1973) or some other proscribed stylistic manual, you will find that they all contain useful instructions regarding captions, which includes the titling of figures, graphs and tables. There is one exception, however, to the APA Manual's instructions and that is that figures, graphs and tables usually appear within the text, rather than at the end, as one does when preparing a paper for publication in a journal. At times, when you are presenting details and voluminous data, your committee may suggest that you move that particular Table to the Appendix, so as to maintain a smoother textual flow.

The general overriding error regarding the captioning of figures, graphs and tables is that insufficient data regarding content is provided. The general principle is that each figure, graph and table should be able to 'stand on its own'!

In the construction of a table, graph, map or chart then, remember that they should be self-contained; i.e., if separated from the body of your writing, the charts, maps, graphs, etc., should speak clearly to a reader—therefore, check all of your titles carefully to be sure that they adequately describe the content. A good procedure for this process is to have someone else go over your list of tables to determine if they make sense out of context. Finally, if you use abbreviations, be sure that you include a legend explaining what the abbreviations represent.

The full captioning of your tables, graphs and figures, should make them self explanatory and your reader should not have to earnestly study the text to make it clear. Again, your dissertation is not intended to be a Gothic romance novel. Tenets of scholarly writing may not make a best seller, but following them is more likely to result in plaudits from your professional audience, not to mention those three letters after your name!

Summaries of Chapters. And after all that 'captioning' you finally arrive at that glorious part of dissertation writing, the summary. The typical chapter summary tends to be a particularly irksome aspect of dissertation writing with your reader left 'nodding off'! So, when you write a summary, please put some "guts" into what you say. For example, in Chapter three, let the reader know in a few specific statements what it is that you are using as a data collection plan of action! Similarly, in the summary section of the review of the literature chapter provide a brief overview of what others have done in relationship to your topic. You must remember that many readers may only have time to read the summaries of some of your chapters. Therefore, give them important facts, data and information; and do the integrative work for them. If your reader has to struggle to make sense of your dissertation chapter, you need to recast your ending summary section (and perhaps the chapter itself!).

There is one additional note to these comments provided in Chapter Two regarding the review of the literature. At the risk of being super redundant it often is usual to write a mini-series of summaries at the end of each section of the literature review, resulting in a major (though brief) summary at the end of this chapter, which ties all the various sections together. Again, your reader should be left with a sense of understanding and expectation of what is to follow.

Preparing the Abstract. After writing the entire dissertation, as noted in Chapter Seven, you will arrive at the formulation of the 'super star' of all the previous summaries, the Abstract. Usually, there is an abstract length requirement (for example, three hundred and fifty words for those dissertations printed by University Microfilms in *Dissertation Abstracts International*). A dissertation abstract *cannot* be any longer than 350 words, because University Microfilms places them on-line. University Microfilms suggests counting the number of characters—including spaces and punctuation marks—in a line of average length and multiplying by the number of lines. A maximum of 2,450 characters will keep you within the limit. Master's abstracts are limited to 250 words. Mathematical formulas, diagrams, and other illustrative materials are never included in the abstract.

Such limitations on length, increase pressures for brevity while maintaining clarity; especially since it is the Abstract of your dissertation which is initially read to get a sense of what your study is about. By way of 'super summarizing', your abstract should contain a succinct statement of the problem, procedures or method followed, the results obtained and their implications.

Do not fill chapters with lengthy details (for example, interview schedules, questionnaires, tests, or detailed interventions, examination procedures, legal documents, etc.). In some cases these may be of interest to the specialist who may want to replicate your study. Details of this order may be put in the appendix. They will not be lost to the few who may want access to them and yet they do not "clutter up" the main thrust of the study. The appendixes (or appendices) are labeled and lettered in order of their appearance in the body of your report. That is, those things that are first mentioned in the body become the first appendix and those that are mentioned later become second, third, etc. List each Appendix by letter and title in the Table of Contents.

The bibliography contains all references found in the text listed in alphabetical order by author. You will use the reference citation style advocated by your field of study and your institution. Every reference appearing in your text should be found listed in your Bibliography. Missing citations may make your entire work suspect. Some institutions list the Bibliography before the Appendices and others reverse the process. You will as always follow local custom.

Stylistic Considerations

Scholarly Writing. It has been my experience that even students who write reasonably well for a specific audience and with a specific focus in mind (e.g., clinical-type case studies for a clinical conference) may encounter some initial and longer lasting difficulties writing in the scholarly style required in dissertations. The preceding, as well as the following comments, are aimed at being helpful to this process. Although there is no easy way to overcome inadequacies in logic or linguistic expression, these pages (particularly, Chapters One, Two and this Chapter; as well as Chapter Eight) describe for you a step-by-step guide to assist you in the process and procedures of completing a dissertation.

It is assumed that you have not only surveyed the literature in your area of study, but that you have gathered together the essential tools of a writer's trade—namely:

. . . manuals of style and form (e.g., Campbell & Ballou, 1982; Mullin, 1977; Ross-Larson, 1982; Strunk & White, 1979; and Zinsser, 1980);

. . . publication guidelines for your field of research (e.g., American Psychological Association, *Publication Manual,* 1983; Modern Language Association, *MLA Handbook for Writers of Research Papers, Theses &*

Dissertations, 1977; and Turabian *A Manual for Writers of Term Papers, Theses & Dissertations,* 1973).

. . . dictionaries, thesaureses and various reference books (such as Roget's *Thesaurus of English Words & Phrases,* 1965; Funk & Wagnall's *Standard Handbook of Synonyms, Antonyms & Prepositions,* 1947; and standard dictionaries;

. . . and of course, a dissertation handbook such as this one (hooray!) (as well as Campbell, Ballou & Slade, 1982; Gardner & Beatty (1980); and Madsen, 1983).

. . . Also refer to Chapters One, Two, Eight and the Appendices.

Suggestions for getting started on formulating and writing the dissertation and for working with the committee also appear in Chapters One, Two, Seven and Eight. These suggestions include writing in small units and then combining and organizing these materials in a chapter format and cataloguing all ideas you have for future research, etc. While writing, remember that you are directing your remarks to a broader audience than your particular discipline. You need to meet not only your advisor's requirements, but also the requirements of a committee which has members from other departments. Furthermore, your thesis may be read by people of other disciplines, and you need to be able to communicate to them also.

Your particular style of dissertation writing will emerge quickly in the initial chapters of your rough draft. Your advisor will try as much as possible to assist you in retaining your style, while at the same time directing you toward good expository writing techniques. You will obviously consult your advisor early in the dissertation formulation and writing process and will consult with her/him as to when to submit your drafts to the other committee members. When the manuscript is finally ready, you will submit it to the committee in its entirety, noting all the aspects required in this transaction, as detailed in Chapters Two, Seven and Eight.

In writing your dissertation your advisor will often recommend that you press on to the first draft of your chapters, realizing that you will have opportunity to improve upon them in future revisions. It is also recommended that you allow yourself sufficient time for the revision process as the usual experience is that you will revise your first draft twice or thrice. It is further advised that you make at least one xerox copy of the early draft which you keep safe from fire, flood or other disaster (e.g., one copy in the refrigerator, another in your family's safety deposit box).

In devising and revising drafts of your dissertation it is helpful to keep in mind that scholarly writing should not leave the reader in doubt as to what you are actually discussing. Therefore you need to delete indefinite and vague expressions, as well as trite or imprecise ones and opt for a clear and direct expression. A common error is to animate the chapter. Remember—chapters do nothing; only you, the researcher does things in the chapter. A guide to more appropriate and direct expression is provided in Strunk & White (1979). A few examples of terms to be avoided are provided below.

As to—here is a phrase that is cumbersome and awkward. Generally the word "to" will suffice alone, or "about" is appropriate.

In terms of—this expression is freely battered about in educational writing. Rewrite the sentence to remove this phrase

Additionally, the use of the indefinite person tends to cause problems in dissertation writing. To be more explicit, you usually do not use pronouns such as "you", "our", and "we" when formulating a thesis. Furthermore, you do not refer to yourself except on rare occasions. Some of you may fall into the habit of stating "the author. . . ." You will be allowed this luxury only a few times in your scientific publications, say, after your third book. There are, however, some notable exceptions to these guidelines, especially when formulating a qualitative type of methodology and in these proposed instances, it is best to consult with your advisor.

Use of Abbreviations. This is a particularly hard topic with which to cope. You may have a situation where you will repeat the name of a concept such as a test throughout the body of your thesis (e.g., Minnesota Multiphasic Personality Inventory (MMPI). When employing such terminology, first provide the full name of the measure and then its acronym (in parentheses). Do so at the beginning of each paragraph using the concept. Then you may merely employ the acronym in the rest of the paragraph. If you do this, be sure that in your summaries, and at the beginning of chapters where you may loose your readers, you repeat the full name and then the acronym (in parentheses). Be merciful in such endeavors because your reader may find her/himself in the position of having to refer back and forth time and time again trying to remember what it is you are about. Saturated wiht abbreviations, reading could be quite a chore! Remember the general principle that *each* chapter, *each* paragraph and *each* table or graph should be able to be understandable, without a reading of the entire text!

Use of Non-Sexist Language. You are expected to employ a non-sexist style of writing in your manuscript. Hence unless impersonal language is used the former 'he' becomes s/he, and 'his' is expressed as her/his.

Use of Tense. Much energy is spent trying to decide what to do about tense in thesis writing. Please follow this procedure! In the dissertation proposal, you will employ the present or future tense for the most part. When you do the final dissertation writing, simply switch the tense of the first three chapters to the past tense as the study is then completed. The parts of the thesis added after the proposal should be the past tense except for the suggestions for future research in the last chapter. Try to avoid compound tenses; they tend to lose their punch. (Of course, this is difficult for the research proposal which is usually present and/or future tenses.)

Errors and the Use of Editorial Assistance. You can be as certain as taxes that some of your committee members will know when the slightest letter is misplaced, inverted or substituted. So beware of misspelling, missing phrases, awkward expression and inappropriate use of words and ideas. You are totally responsible for the accuracy of your copy. If you have trouble, seriously consider hiring an editor (and don't forget there are such aids as a dictionary). Editors can serve a useful function in assisting you to more adequate expression.

Preparing the Manuscript for the Library

The following comments are directed particularly to the preparation of the final dissertation. They may be useful when preparing the proposal and as a preface to the final copy presentation. You also need to check out your institution's specific requirements for preparing and filing your theses. Many graduate schools and/or graduate library personnel provide pamphlets detailing such considerations as paper, typing, margins, the use of illustrations and photographs, etc. All the following comments dealing with this subject are merely meant to be suggestions and local institutional requirements need to be determined and followed.

Typing. Typing must be on one side of the paper only. Double-space all textual material and all preliminary pages. Footnotes and long quotations may be single-spaced. Pica, elite, or book-faced type may be used, but whichever your choice, use it consistently. It is wise to provide your typist with a new ribbon, a clean typewriter, and a copy of this guide. If your typist has access to one of the fantastic new correcting typewriters, your difficulties in achieving an absolutely perfect original manuscript are solved. If, however, you are in the great majority, the problems are greater. *No* erasures or crossed out material can appear on the finished product; however, the use of liquid paper is allowed. It does not show up in microfilming and photocopying as erasures do. Used judiciously (two very thin coats, each allowed to dry thoroughly), it is quite unobtrusive even in the original manuscript.

Dissertations are microfilmed exactly as they are received from a University, neither edited nor retyped. Thus, your manuscript must be error-free and well set up, since it represents not only you, but your university. Negative microfilm of each dissertation will remain at University Microfilms so that other scholars may order positive microfilm, microfiche, or xerographic copies in time to come. Thus, the selection of a first-rate typist is crucial. Your departmental administrative officer may contain the names of reputable typists, familiar with their rules and regulations. You would be wise to secure these references.

Photocopying. You may need to present the original manuscript and one clear, clean copy to the library. However, in cases where the original has been altered many times, and is showing wear-and-tear, two clear immaculate copies may be submitted if they meet the University Microfilms and your institutional Library standards.

Much of your success in obtaining good copy is determined by the quality of your photocopy. There are many photocopiers in any area—choose one with a good reputation; make sure the operator knows the proper weight and rag content paper you want (the same as your original copy); insist on perfect copy. You may discover an outlet that charges less than the average, but the quality of work does not justify the meagre saving. After all the research and preparation you have already put into your dissertation, it hardly makes sense to risk poor results to save a very small amount.

Permission to Use Previously Copyrighted Material. If you are using material copyrighted by another, either in the main body or appendices, you *must* obtain permission for its use, and indicate this in a footnote on the first page of the material. The use of material without permission delays the microfilming and exposes you to possible legal action by the person holding the copyright. If you are quoting several lines of an authority to strengthen a point you are making, it is not necessary to write for permission. In this case, simply footnote your source properly.

University Microfilms. You are required to sign an agreement with University Microfilms when your dissertation is ready for microfilming. This agreement authorizes the microfilming of the dissertation and the publishing of the abstract, and releases University Microfilms from any obligation if there is any copyright violation in the dissertation. The agreement form must be accompanied by a xerox copy of the title page.

The candidate may also, at the same time, request that University Microfilms copyright her/his dissertation, by indicating this wish on the agreement form. This same form is used in requesting reprints of the candidate's abstract.

A pamphlet entitled "Preparing Your Dissertation for Microfilming" which includes useful information about copyrighting is published by University Microfilms. Copies of this publication are usually available at the graduate office of the candidate's school as well as at Reference Services of your university library.

Summary and Overview

In the preceding paragraphs, organizational and stylistic considerations in reference to dissertation preparation were presented. These included topics such as: the usual order of presentation, the use of captions, introductory and summarizing paragraphs, scholarly writing and preparing the manuscript for the library. In the following chapters, various types of research methodology, the use of a statistical consultant, developmental difficulties in dissertating, the preparation of the final dissertation chapters, as well as life after the dissertation, will be presented so that the reader may successfully master the dissertation process and satisfactorily complete the dissertation.

Chapter Four

Research Design: Experimental and Quasi-Experimental

Joseph Reimer, Ed.D.

At the heart of the dissertation stands the research study itself. After choosing a topic and reviewing the literature, you come to the moment of truth—when you must describe in some detail the plan of your study. This is what the committee in your hearing probably will focus most attention on; for it is in the detail of your plan, or research design, that lies the potential richness and validity of your study.

Research Design

As the term suggests, research needs to be designed. To be sure, in real life much of research happens unexpectedly, even serendipitously. But to take advantage of the unexpected, one must have a firm sense of plan or design. Without it you risk two unfortunate scenarios: the non-ending dissertation which goes on and on without closure, and the misunderstood dissertation which is fought over in committee because no one has a clear idea of what had been proposed. The design functions simultaneously as guide for you in wandering through the collection and analysis of your data and as contract between you and your readers as to what minimally must be delivered for you to have satisfactorily completed this requirement.

Concomitantly, the research design assures the scientific validity of your work. In the words of Fred Kerlinger, it is "the plan, structure and strategy of investigation conceived so as to obtain answers to research questions and to control variance" (1973, p. 300). By "plan" is meant the outline of activities to be undertaken, by "structure" the outline of variables to be studied and by "strategy" the methods to be used to gather and analyze the data.

Research Questions

A research design begins with research questions. You come to your study with a set of questions for which you will be seeking answers, however tentative, and the design guides you in finding answers. But the answers can only be as good as the questions which open the study.

Formulating the questions, or the problem, is an art in its own right. The questions ought genuinely to spring from your native curiosity, for it is your interest in exloring them that has to sustain your efforts throughout. But the questions which first come tumbling from our minds are often like diamonds in the rough. They need to be cut and shined before they can properly sit atop of a research design.

As an example, let us take a question current in the field of adult development, "How do friendships between women differ from friendships between men?" The question is based on a common observation that women in our culture tend to be more intimate with same-sex friends than are men who tend to be more active with same-sex friends. The question assumes differences and seeks a description ("how") of them.

Though there is much to recommend a question of current interest, this is as yet a question in the rough. It is not yet testable or answerable. First, unless there are previous studies which have already established that the assumed differences do observably exist, it is a mistake to build the assumption into the question and move directly to describing the phenomenon. Better to openmindedly test for the assumed differences ("do these friendships differ?") and avoid untested assumptions. Second, the terms of the question are unclear and beg for definition. What is meant by "friendship", how are they assumed "to differ", and of which "women" and "men" are we speaking? Until each of the key terms of a research question is clearly defined, it is impossible to proceed with designing the research plan.

Let us look at the term "friendship" to see what is meant by clear definition. Obviously one person's "friendship" is another person's "acquaintance", for we have multiple ways in our culture of defining this relationship, and even the dictionary is not going to be helpful. The researcher is faced with coming up with a definition which is neither so broad as to be non-discriminating nor so limited as to appear arbitrary or idiosyncratic. What is wanted is a definition which is compatible with previous definitions in the literature of the field, which will commonly fit experiences of the subjects of the study and which is open to being operationalized. You want to be sure that other scholars will recognize and accept your definition, that the women and men in the study will commonly "have" friendships that will fit the definition and that features of the relationships (such as duration, frequency, intensity) can be observed and measured so that the proposed "differences" can be tested through the research design.

The Major Variables

Another way of getting clear about research questions is to think of whether they are clearly setting forth a proposed relationship between the major variables of the study.

In our example, the major variables are gender (male/female) and friendship. What is being asked is whether certain features of friendship (to be defined) vary by gender. Gender is the independent variable: the one that is given. Friendship is the dependent variable: the one that is said to vary in relationship to the variance in the independent variable.

Every study will have major variables, though not every one will have definable independent versus dependent variables. (You may wish to study variables that co-vary or correlate where neither can be said to depend upon the other for its variance. Often this is a matter of perception, but translates into the use of different statistics and modes of interpretation. What need be seen is that in calling the phenomena under study "variables", we are assuming that; (1) in real life they vary or fluctuate; (2) in ways that can be observed and measured; and (3) we can account for the fluctuation (or some proportion of it) in terms of the relationship between the phenomena.

In our example the independent variable varies categorically in terms of female and male. (It varies by category and not continuously by numerical score or rank order.) We will not have to worry about measuring the variance, nor will we be able to increase the variance (unless we were to add another category such as "cross-sex" friendships). We therefore turn to the dependent variable to maximize our within-study variance. If we have properly defined "friendship" and have decided to select as its features to study "frequency of contact" and "intimacy of dialogue", we have to define these features in ways that are clear, consistent and admit of variation. By the last we mean that they can be observed to systematically vary in either categorical or continuous terms. The friendships will vary continuously in the number of times the friends contact one another per month and categorically in degree of intimacy that typifies their conversations. We want to maximize the variance in the dependent variable to allow for adequate differences by gender to emerge.

Control of Variance

The selecting of major variables is actually making a bold statement. It is saying that of all the possible influences on the fluctuation of a given phenomenon (e.g., intimacy of friendship dialogue), there is one influence (gender) that can account for a significant proportion of the fluctuation. The statement would remain incredible were it not for a solid research design that could assure control of extraneous variance and valid methods and measures for gathering and analyzing the data on the desirable variance.

The extraneous variance refers to the influence of all other possible independent variables on the dependent variable that have not been defined as part of the study. In our example we might imagine that besides gender, variables such as age, socio-economic status and interpersonal style of friends as well as duration and continuity of friendship may influence the "frequency of contact" and "intimacy of dialogue." A major function of research design is to control for these types of extraneous variables so that we can say with confidence that their possible presence in our study is not "contaminating", or overlapping with, the relationship between variables which we have isolated for study.

There are three ways of controlling variance: by eliminating the variables, by building them into the design and by randomizing the assignment of subjects and conditions. The first two have to do with selection of sample and the third with that and methodology (which we will deal with below).

Sample Selection

Who we pick to study is a major issue in design as is how we approach and relate to our subjects.

The question of "who" has largely to do with availability of subjects, but has immediate impact on control of variance. Given limited funds and time (an almost universal condition of graduate studies in the 1980's), you will probably end up studying subjects to whom you have some direct access. They may be students in a school or university with which you are affiliated or members of an organization with which you have contact or residents of an area near where you live. All these are acceptable routes for contacting subjects, but they impose limitations on your study of which you need be aware.

In our example, we ideally would want to include a broad cross-section of American women and men in order to test the effect in our culture of gender on friendship. But since this usually will not be possible, we have to be conscious of how the limitations of our sample affect our results. If the study were carried out with alumni of a university between the ages of 30 and 35 and living in the Pacific Northwest, we would immediately understand that the results could not properly be generalized to men and women of another age bracket, educational background and region of the country or globe, for our sample would not be representative of those populations. But on the positive side, by selecting this defined population, we have *ipso facto* eliminated much extraneous variance. What we lost in generalizability, we have gained in terms of assuring that age, region and educational level are not contaminating variables.

Since, however, it is likely that the alumni of a given university who volunteer to be part of a study on friendship have characteristics (demographic, personal and situational) which are not necessarily shared by a larger population of people of even the same age, region and educational background, we have to consider both what these may be and how, as independent variables operating extraneously in our study, they may be affecting the variance of our dependent variable.

One such characteristic is the fact of their being volunteers. It is not unreasonable to assume that people who freely volunteer to give information about a given topic are comfortable with it and may have had more experience with

38

or given more thought to it than most other people of the same population. Other characteristics may be marital status, profession, religion, ethnicity, intellectual level or interpersonal style. The point is to have a mechanism in place by which we can identify what characteristics may characterize and skew our sample and how these may be extraneously operating in the study. A good place to start is with previous studies of adult friendships to see what their authors have identified as possibly significant independent variables.

After eliminating some extraneous variance through limiting certain sample characteristics, we can further eliminate variance by using a randomized selection process. If it were possible to get a list of all the alumni of certain classes and to randomly select a pool of subjects to whom we would turn to participate in the study, we would be assured that the major demographic and personal characteristics would be better controlled through the randomized selection. Further, if we had a large pool of volunteers and could randomly select of those who would actually participate in the study, the variance would be even better controlled.

Barring the preferable possibility of randomization, we are faced with the harder and less satisfying choice of eliminating more variance and building some into the study. We might decide that marital status and intellectual level play a role in affecting the dependent variable. With marital staus we decide, given that a large percentage of the sample pool is married, to eliminate it as a variable and thereby limit the study to only those alumni, female and male, who are in an on-going marriage of a year's duration or more. With intellectual level, though, we are more curious to know its effect, and hence decide to build it into the study, for example, by asking for college board scores and cumulative grade point average. We then devise a di- or tri-chotomous rating of "intellectual level" and divide the men and women into those levels, creating a more complex research design, but controlling more of the variance. We probably would not build in too many such variables, for with each one included, we necessitate the enlarging of our sample. For practical reasons, eliminating variables is often the chosen course.

Treatment of Subjects

Once we have selected a pool of possible subjects, we need to bear in mind certain methodological procedures and ethical considerations in approaching and relating to them.

As mentioned in Chapter 2, every subject has a right to informed consent. He or she has a right to know what to expect by agreeing to participate, particularly in terms of time commitment, nature of participation, possible negative experiences and potential benefits. This is standardly written up by the researcher and signed by the subject *before* participation begins. The subject, however, is usually not informed as to the specific major variables under study or the hypothesized outcomes. This is to assure that he or she is not influenced to give responses considered desirable for reaching certain outcomes.

Perhaps more subtle, but even more significant, is the question of our attitude towards the subjects. We may indeed view them as "subjects"; that is, people who are subject to our will as researcher. Perhaps in our zeal to produce objective results, we decide to tell them as little as possible and to be as neutral as possible in our interaction with them. The danger here, though, is that the subjects sense our distance and have little incentive to be involved in the study and even resent our control over them (see Argyris, 1980).

The alternative perhaps worth considering is to see subjects as collaborators. True, they need remain blind to our hypotheses; but given that "blindness", we may still communicate a sense that they are experts about their own experience, for example, of friendships, and that we are turning to them to share as accurately as possible their expertise with us. Without violating the cannons of objectivity, we may yet empower our subjects and give them what even money cannot buy, our respect for their experience and intelligence. After the study is completed, we may return and share with them what we have learned, getting their feedback on that. Thus the study becomes a circle of learning in which they and we both participate and contribute.

Methodologies

Following Kerlinger (1973) we have arrived now at the questions of strategies or methods for gathering and analyzing of data. We are faced with some broad choices of methods or approaches and some more specific choices of techniques for observing and instruments in measuring. On the broader choice, Kerlinger presents two basic approaches: experimental and ex post facto. We will look at these in reverse order and divide the experimental into "true experiments" and "quasi experiments."

Ex-Post Facto Research

As the term suggests, ex post facto research deals with variables which have already occurred before the study began. Our example of studying friendship fits well. All the subjects whom we would be studying have already been in friendships before we approach them or else they would not be in the study.

If you are wondering why this factor is so significant, it is because in a study of this sort we have no direct control over the variables, which leaves us at a scientific disadvantage. We have to take the variables as they come, and for all efforts to control extraneous variance, we can only partially succeed. Friendships vary for a host of reasons, and we will be able to account for only a small percentage of the variance.

What is a weakness is also a strength. If you are interested in studying phenomena as they occur *over time* in people's lives—such as friendships, marriage, success in school or at work, you have to realize these variables cannot be created instantaneously in a laboratory experiment. They only come in the rough and have to be studied ex post facto.

Built into this type of research is an inherent caution: because as investigator you cannot manipulate or essentially control the variables you are studying, your conclusions are based on inference and need be limited. In our example, we may find from a concomitant variation of our major variables, gender and features of friendship, that there is a statistically significant relationship between them. What our results mean, though, is not that variation in gender causes, or fully accounts for, the variation in friendship, but that some percentage of the variation in friendship is accounted for by gender. In other words, differences in friendship are not caused by being female or male, but tend to be associated with gender, and the rest of the story remains clouded.

What is crucial in this type of research is care in selection of sample (as outlined above), use of valid and reliable instruments (see below) and testing of alternative hypotheses. To stress the last, we need to remember that good research involves only tentative commitment to even our most cherished assumptions, read hypotheses. We need always remain open to the possibility that things happen quite differently than our hypotheses would predict. We may assume that women tend to be more intimate than men in friendship, but we need to frame our research in such a way that not only the null hypothesis (that there are no differences between the sexes in intimacy of friendship) may stand, but also that the alternative hypothesis (that men tend to be more intimate) may be proven true. Even if the hypothesis as stated received confirmation, we need remember that alternative explanations, having to do with extraneous variance, remain plausible: it may not be gender alone, but other factors as well, that account for the results.

Instruments. Which instruments to use remains a choice specifically determined by the phenomenon under study and what is available for observing it and measuring its variation. What can be commented on in general are the issues of validity and reliability and the tension between using standardized versus homemade instruments.

Validity refers to the truth value of an instrument while reliability refers to its consistency in usage. A valid instrument is one which measures what it says it does: a claim not easily established. In our study while it may not be difficult to get a valid record of how often friends contact one another, it may be more difficult to get a reading of intimacy. How does one know that a measure of intimacy in fact gets at intimacy rather than a host of other factors of friendship?

To claim an instrument is reliable means it will perform consistently from time one to time two and in the hands of different scorers. Theoretically an instrument may prove reliable, but not be valid (it may consistently measure some other phenomena); practically, a high reliability reinforces our sense of the instrument's validity.

In ex post facto research we face a tension around using standardized instruments. Their standardization increases their reliability, and often, they have stood the test of validity. That recommends their use for they lend credibility to the study. But since they were designed for purposes other than this study, they may be they may be measuring a phenomenon other than what is being studied. For example, in our study we may choose to use a measure of intimacy normed on married couples, and not on friends, because it is standardized. Our alternative is to create an instrument of our own based on friendship data. The advantage is the closeness of fit. The problem is: how can we establish its validity if this is its first usage? Getting good reliability is a partial answer, but the problem stands and the tension remains. A not bad compromise is to use both types of instruments and discuss the similarities and differences in results.

Experimental Research

An experiment is "a scientific investigation in which an investigator manipulates and controls one or more independent variables and observes the dependent variable(s) for variation concomitant to the manipulation of the independent variables" (Kerlinger, 1973, p. 315).

The element of control and manipulation stands out in this type of research precisely because its scientific ideal is to get as pure a reading as possible of the relation between identified variables and to keep extraneous variance to a minimum. This ideal is achieved by randomization of subjects and treatments, operationalization of variables, and valid and precise measurement of variation.

Sample selection is not as crucial to this type of research for once a sample pool is gathered, the subjects are randomly assigned to treatment or experimental groups, or if groups are intact, they are randomly assigned to the experimental condition. Randomization takes care of much of the extraneous variance, for whatever extraneous characteristics subjects bring to the study, they are distributed randomly among groups or treatments.

Operationalizing of variables refers to the translation of more abstract variables into concretely observable behaviors. An excellent example of this process comes from Milgram's (1974) rather controversial experiments on obedience to authority. Obedience is the type of variable one might think of studying in an ex post facto design as a given characteristic of persons (such as "the authoritarian personality"). Milgram's genius, in a tradition of social-psychological experiments on conformity, was to operationalize obedience as occuring in a situation "in which one person orders another person to perform an observable action" and to experimentally create that situation so as to make concretely observable "when obedience to the imperative occurs and when it fails to occur" (p. 13). In the situation Milgram created, subjects came into a lab told that they were to participate in an experiment on learning through the punishing of error, but were actually being observed (unbeknown to them—which is the controversy) for whether they would obey the authority of the lab technician and continue administering electric shock to an innocent victim beyond the point where he would be (were the shock really administered) intensely pained.

By dramatically creating a situation which called for obedience against the "normal" moral impulse not to hurt an innocent person, Milgram tried to build real life tension into an otherwise artificial laboratory situation. The movie version of these experiments confirm that he succeeded, suggesting a situation in which subjects truly believed they faced an authority who was ordering them to perform the punishing action. The experimental question was whether they would obey or refuse to obey, but the choice point could be precisely measured because each subject was sitting in front of an instrument panel consisting of 30 lever switches with a voltage designation that ranged from 15 to 450 volts. The instructions were to increase the voltage by 15 volts after each mistake that the "learner" made in learning trial (which was the cover for the real experiment). At some point before reaching 450 volts the subjects could refuse to go on with the learning trial and despite orders from the authority to continue, they could discontinue the experiment. That point was the concrete measure of their refusal to obey, which created the scientific advantage of not having to rely on subjects' reports of when they would have refused, but rather on a measured observation of when they did, or did not, refuse to obey. As Milgram claims and attempts to demonstrate, people consistently overestimated how strong their and other people's will to resist would be, for subjects were far less likely to resist authority than any one had predicted before the experiment was run.

Besides the advantage that the experimental methodology provided in creating unambiguous measures of obedience and disobedience, it also allowed Milgram to manipulate the independent variables by creating 16 different experimental situations and to control for extraneous variance by randomly assigning subjects to the different treatment conditions. Thus he could show, for example, that level of obedience varied significantly by the proximity to the subject of the victim and the authority. The closer the victim and the further away the authority, the greater the tendency of subjects to refuse to obey. It would have been exceedingly difficult to have shown this relationship between proximity and obedience in ex post facto research for the subjects were not aware of proximity as a factor to report and the investigator would not have been present to consistently observe this relationship as one can in an experimental situation.

To summarize, the advantages of creating a "true" experiment is the control of extraneous variance, the manipulation of internal variance and the precise and valid measure of the operationalized dependent variable. The disadvantages are the lack of observation over time, the removal of subjects from their natural environment and, ethically speaking, the inability to treat subjects as collaborators in the research effort.

Quasi-Experimental Design

"If the experimenter does not have the power either to assign subjects to experimental groups or to assign experimental treatments to the groups, this study may be an experiment, but not a *true* experiment" (Kerlinger, 1973, p. 315).

The power to randomize assignment, which for Kerlinger underlies the methodology of the true experiment, is not always available, especially for those involved in evaluation research. The effort to systematically evaluate the outcomes, and worthwhileness, of new programs or interventions often operates within the real-life restrictions of non-random assignment to groups. Researchers often are called to evaluate programs after they have already begun, and have to evaluate groups that had been formed not by random assignment, but by the rhythms of daily life.

Can scientific research be done under these conditions? This is a question explored by Campbell and Stanley in their famous monograph, *Experimental and Quasi-Experimental Designs for Research* (1963). While they, as Kerlinger, argue for the scientific advantages of true experimental design where random assignment rules the day, they also make provisions for quasi-experimental designs which, while not perfect, do avoid the pitfalls of scientific invalidity.

As an example we will look at their number 10: "the non-equivalent control group design" (p. 47), which they diagram as follows:

$$\frac{0 \quad - \quad X \quad - \quad 0 \quad -}{0 \quad - \quad \quad \quad - \quad 0 \quad -}.$$

Involved here are two previously intact groups, such as two classes of the same grade and approximately the same ability-level and socio-economic level, where the researcher is able to *randomly* assign treatment X to one of the two groups and use the other as a control group which does not receive that treatment. Previous to the beginning of the treatment both groups are pre-tested on a valid measure of whatever is the dependent variable (the skill in quality that is to be affected by the treatment), and subsequent to the treatment both are re-tested to see if there has been a change in the scores. What the control group, the random assignment of treatment and the pre and post testing allow for is enough control of variance so that if the experimental groups scores go up significantly more than the scores of the control group, the difference may be attributed to the effects of treatment and not random variation.

Please note that if there were no control group, there would be no way of knowing if the gain scores of the target group were due to the treatment, or to chance. Were the two groups not approximately comparable in external characteristics and historical circumstance (being in the same grade, school and universe at the same time in history), the validity of the results would be weakened. Were the treatment not randomly assigned, but were one group to volunteer for it while the other decided not to volunteer, the validity of the results would again be weakened. For the principle remains: the more the quasi-experiment approaches a true experiment, controlling extraneous variance, the more confidence we can have in its results.

Your own evaluation research may lack the possibility of random assignment of treatment since you came truly after-the-fact. Do not worry; you are not alone in doing ex post facto evaluation research. As long as you do arrive on time to set up a believable control group and to pre and post-test the dependent variable in both groups, your results will usually be acceptable. Two further points of consideration: you may want to set up a post-post test several weeks or months after the conclusion of the treatment to test whether the positive effects had some permanence; and, if you believe in your program, you may want to offer the control group an opportunity to experience it after the testing is complete. That makes good ethical sense as well as allowing for properly treating a totally volunteer population. Half would be randomly selected (immediately) get the treatment and the other half would serve as controls while waiting their turn. At the end, though, everyone—including you the researcher—would have gotten full benefit.

References

Argyris, C. (1980). *Inner contradictions of rigorous research*. New York: Academic Press.

Campbell, D. T., and Stanley, J. C. (1963). *Experimental and quasi-experimental designs for research*. Chicago: Rand McNally.

Kerlinger, F. N. (1973). *Foundations of behavioral research* (2nd). New York: Holt, Rinehart & Winston.

Milgram, S. (1974). *Obedience to authority*. New York: Harper & Row.

Chapter Five

Research Design: Qualitative Research: The Discipline and the Technique

Hilary E. Bender, Ph.D.
Boston University

Gallia est omnis divisa . . . : Setting the Context

Although there are as many research methods as there are researchers, we can, like Caesar, conveniently group them into three types: theoretic, qualitative and experimental. The theoretic researcher using the oldest and most common method, draws on library or archival materials. Beginning with premises found in the literature,—ideas or theories already established—and proceeding logically and critically, he or she argues toward new conclusions. This researcher seeks to persuade you to a new view of truth by the careful marshalling of sources, by a precision of thinking, and by the strength of the logic displayed. To the theoretic researcher, truth lies behind the mask of sense data, 'the deceptive appearance of things,' and is to be found in the hidden essences of reality; truth can be apprehended only through the mind's rational powers.

> *Comment:* Theoretic research is at its best in the humanities, especially philosophy. It is also used in the human sciences but with less satisfaction. Words reflecting human experience are less than exact; they lack the precision required by logic. Moreover, the 'truth' of human behavior is sometimes other than logical.

Experimental (quantitative or statistical) research turns from the above base, what we 'think' things to be, back to the outside world as it is reported by our senses, 'the observable and the measurable.' It respects the objective world and sees it as unified and orderly. The task of the researcher is to discover this order—its 'laws'—for purposes of definition, but also for prediction and control. To accomplish this discovery, the researcher carefully isolates her/his attention to a few specific 'variables,' controlling or putting on hold the influence of all surrounding variables. These selected variables are then manipulated in relation to each other to test, and hopefully prove, the influence one has on the other. If done well, the results apply, not to this specific case alone, but to all identical sets of variables throughout the universe. And as each of these established scientific facts accumulate with many others, the orderly, predictable process of the objective world is gradually revealed.

> *Comment:* Experimental research is at its best in the physical sciences but it too has been beneficially adapted to the human sciences. However, the human experience is highly complex and interdependent, and the isolation and control of single sets of variables is near impossible. Moreover, many have observed in humans an additional phenomenon—sometimes called the human will—which seems to transcend scientific 'laws' and predictability.

The qualitative researcher focuses on the human experience and defines 'truth' as a human phenomenon. It is not just 'out there' as reported by my senses, and not just 'in my mind' as my thinking processes apprehend it, but it interdepends between both. My experience of the outside world is reported to me through my senses in an extraordinarily rich and complex manner, far beyond my reflective awareness. However, as I receive these complex reports, my mind 'makes sense' of them, i.e. it organizes this vast array of data into a single, understandable form. I not only experience my world, I 'understand' it—I give it meaning.

But this is only half the picture; to the qualitative researcher, truth is a two sided interaction. Not only do I interpretively pattern my experience, but I then communicate and confirm these meanings back into my everyday world. A 'chair,' 'Shirley,' her 'depression,' this 'class,' 'Massachusetts,'—all exist as units of reality, as much 'out there' as 'in my mind,' but requiring both orders for their existence.

Moreover, this 'form' giving is as much a social phenomenon as it is an individual one. The social order which preceded me has already richly imbedded these forms into my world before I ever encountered it. They lie hidden but give shape and purpose to all of my life experiences. The task of the qualitative researcher is to carefully search the world as it presents itself, reading each material expression as if it were a sign, and attempt to rediscover these underlying but informing patterns or meanings.

Given this theoretic view, the qualitative researcher wants to *understand* unique *human experiences* and to share both the understanding and the process of understanding with the reader. Rather than seeking to test and prove an idea already assumed, or to argue and persuade the reader to an idea already held, the researcher's intent is to explore and discover the unifying form of some relatively unknown human experience, personal or social. He or she gives the reader both a detailed description of the significant expressions of that human phenomenon along with the underlying pattern of the perceived meaning that has been identified. This permits the reader to decide as to how faithful the researcher's interpretation is when compared to the phenomenon itself.

Comment: Ordinarily, we see 'truth' as a one-to-one match between a term and the phenomenon it refers to; a term is either true or false. However, in qualitative thinking, a term (concept or theory) is *analogous* to the reality it reflects. It identifies and organizes the reality, but in doing so, it also selectively simplifies the reality's complexity and layers of nuances. A concept can never be totally adequate to the reality it presents, only relatively so. Therefore, there is no one correct interpretation, and the results of a piece of qualitative research are not true or false, but either superficial and contrived, or deeply *faithful* to the reality they attempt to reveal.

Qualitative research is judged on two criteria: clarity and credibility. The first criterion asks how clear and memorable is the researcher's interpretation? An interpretation needs *Praegnanz* as the Gestalt psychologists term it: an inventive balance between simplicity and adequacy. The second, credibility, refers to the faithful correlation the reader experiences between the interpretation and the data out of which it emerged: was the interpretation somewhat invented and imposed or did it truly emerge out of and reflect the true form of the data?

Comment: The qualitative researcher can not claim that the results of one study are predictively generalizable to all similar situations. Each human experience is considered unique as is each research effort. While patterns emerge, 'laws' of behavior and predictions do not. On the other hand, readers frequently acknowledge that a good piece of qualitative research offers striking insights into many comparative human situations.

In major contrast to the norm of objectivity of quantitative research, striving to eliminate all 'contaminating' influence of the researcher, the qualitative researcher gains understanding only through his or her presence and participation—only through the human engagement of the phenomenon in its natural setting, in all its complexity and contextuality, and only through the researcher's unique response to that phenomenon. Rather than deny or eliminate it, the researcher consciously acknowledges the particular perspective and conscious selectivity of his or her engagement; it is the heart of this research method. On the other hand, the researcher must never loose objectivity and become confused or overwhelmed by the experience under study. The level of 'participation' must never go beyond a clear sense of 'self.' Keeping one's balance is one of the major disciplines of this method.

A second discipline can be mentioned at this point. Ordinarily, our mind's process of understanding is spontaneous and unreflected. As much as possible, the researcher seeks to raise this process to a conscious level, i.e. to become aware of the multifarious descriptive details reported by the senses, to consciously and carefully make the many selective choices required to focus on this human experience, and to carefully nurture the process which leads from descriptive details to orderly patterning to formative understanding. This too is a rigor of the qualitative approach.

Contrasting these three general types of research is not to pit one against the other in a battle for ascendency. Each offers a different kind of knowledge; each is appropriate in cases where the other two would be less suitable. Qualitative research methods should be chosen when the researcher wishes to look rigorously at some human experience in context and to describe that experience in detail, for the purpose of a deeper understanding of the form that gives that experience meaning. However, if one wishes to test phenomenon we already understand and raise our certitude to a scientific level, a quantitative method should be chosen. Or if the intention is to critically marshall arguments and thereby persuade the reader to a new perspective, a new 'truth,' the theoretic approach should be used. Both of these latter objectives are good and produce valuable knowledge; neither can be served credibly by using qualitative techniques.

Within the limits of a chapter, the above is intended to serve as a rationale for qualitative research and provided a reasonable base for understanding the various specific techniques and disciplines to follow. From here, the plan is to 'walk through' the research process as if it were a linear procedure. Actually, it undulates back and forth from one step to another, but this will be explained as we proceed.

Specific Techniques

The Focal Quest. Your research task begins by defining to yourself and to your reader the precise human experience you wish to research and by building around that specific focus sufficient context for your reader to clearly understand. This touches a major principle in the method: all understanding is contextual; we understand a particular focal phenomenon only when it is properly placed and interrelated with its background frame of reference. This point would be obvious except that we seldom give conscious notice to this supporting context and tend to 'see' only the focal point. This requires the qualitative researcher to develop the discipline of noting carefully and describing in detail the contextual elements as well as the focal interest.

> *Example:* You are presently focusing on the black markings and printed words of this article. However, you could not see them except in the context of the white paper on which they are printed. You actually are seeing both, white paper and black print, but aware only of the focal point.

Just as you cannot research without identifying your context, neither should you attempt researching without identifying a specific focal point, at least tentatively. No one can 'see' in general, but will unconsciously supply a focal point if not given. Experience shows, however, that an intentional selection of a tentative focal point will allow you to experience the entire situation more clearly. Once you have become oriented to the human experience through the initial focus, you can then reselect and switch to a more relevant organizer.

The Researcher's Position in Relation to the Experience. At some point, you should share with the reader the interests or motivations which lead you to this topic, your degree of experience with it, and your level of involvement or non-involvement in the situation. To what degree are you a participant and to what degree an observer? Share also whatever theoretic or professional perspectives you hold and will use in your examination of this topic. Rather than minimizing and eliminating researcher influence, the qualitative discipline requires elevating it to a conscious level and disclosing it to your reader. This practice not only enables you to redirect unconscious bias, but it reveals to your reader your unique perspective on the experience you are studying. Your perspective represents half the research equation. For these reasons, I recommend the use of the first person 'I' in the writing of your report.

> *Example:* Look at a front-page newspaper photograph and notice how much the angle of the camera, its distance from the subject and the choice of the precise moment 'shapes' the message of the photo. Upon reflection, you will notice that the attitude of the photographer is as much a part of the resulting photograph as is the object he chose to photograph.
>
> In like manner, qualitative research is actually a dialogue between the researcher and the subject being researched . . . and both participants of this dialogue should be disclosed to the awareness and judgment of the reader.

Primary Mode of Research. Once your focal quest is identified, there are several decisions to be made before you begin engaging the field. The first is to choose your primary mode of engaging this experience. Three avenues are open to the qualitative approach: participant-observation, interviewing, and documents. The latter include letters and other written accounts, but extend to photographs, drawings, videos, dream records or any other stable expression or 'account' of human experience. (History and Archeology are good examples of disciplines utilizing qualitatively human 'documents' of the past.) While no one of these three modes is used exclusively, the dominance of one will characterize your study.

Once this primary mode is selected, you will lay out a research plan: a written, detailed—but tentative—strategy that can be followed from initial engagement of the field to final analysis of your material. On one hand, such a plan facilitates and directs your study, avoiding confusion and loss of momentum; on the other, you will hold it as tentative, continually modifying it as you meet immediate situations and make first hand responses to them.

50

Comment: This hints to the primary rhythm of the qualitative method: detailed articulation, than a 'suspension' of this articulation and an intentional openness to the field experience, followed by a new, improved articulation. This undulating pattern is followed throughout the research process and is intentionally disciplined by the researcher who stretches himself at each point—verbalizing as fully and precisely as possible—then intentionally suspending all verbalized assumptions with abandonment to the experience once again, allowing it to speak with minimal prejudgment and maximum freedom—and finally returning to a new articulation, an even more detailed and precise account of the experience understudy. This process is continually repeated throughout the entire study.

Emic or Etic? A second choice is to be made to shape the overall character of your research plan. Borrowing from the linguist's distinction between 'phonemic' and 'phonetic,' the anthropologist describes two polarities of design possibility, 'emic' and 'etic.' The former is more open ended and seeks to discover and reproduce in verbal form the unique perspective of reality lived by your subject(s). Its approach is more sensitive to the emotional complexity of human nature as it is experienced. The etic, on the other hand, is more prestructured, cognitive and informational. It attempts to draw up a cognitive map of a setting it assumes to be orderly and categorical in itself.

The emic is more suitable for exploring personal and cultural experiences which are quite different from our own frame of reference, such as the punk-rock culture, the pattern of experience of a Jewish-Wasp intermarriage, or the experience of a mother of a seriously disturbed child. The etic is better suited for studying semi-familiar or more structured institutional settings, such as administrational styles of leadership, a high school computer program, or the employment patterns of graduates of a media program.

These two approaches are 'polarities,' i.e. every design falls somewhere between the two stereotypes and remains somewhat unique. This article utilizes them to facilitate discussion and clarify your alternatives. Each approach offers its own pattern of interviewing, of conducting participant observation, and its own approach to analysis. It even offers alternatives for the format of your report.

Formats. The emic report often places the heart of the research account 'up front,' extensively recreating the human experience through narrative. Often times the experience will be presented in autobiographic form, using the subject's first person 'I,' and allowing him or her to tell his or her own story. This 'story,' however, will have been extensively organized and edited by the researcher to intensify and simplify its meaning. Following this ethnographic account, the researcher will append a document articulating (1) the focal question of the study with the necessary context, (2) the researcher's journal of the research process and selective choices, and (3) the researcher's inter-

51

pretation of the experience, followed by (4) any commentary the researcher feels worth sharing with the reader.

The etic approach, follows a more standard research format which is outlined as follows:

Ch. 1: focal question with its supporting context and definitions, accompanied by the motivation urging this research effort and giving it value.

Ch. 2: the theoretic perspective through which this experience will be studied.

Ch. 3: the researcher's methodological journal.

Ch. 4: analysis, i.e. the organized presentation of the data.

Ch. 5: synthesis, i.e. the researcher's interpretive theory of the experience.

Ch. 6: commentary: critiques, implications or applications which the researcher adds to the research conclusions.

In any case, you need initially to develop a format on which you will present your research. The formats above, and the basic emic-etic models, have no established value—one is not better than the other. The decision to be made is to determine, in your judgment, the most appropriate and effective way to discover and represent the human experience you are studying.

Theoretic Perspective. A third pre-decision involves the theoretic 'glasses' you will wear as you study this human experience. Will you, the researcher, look and analyze this experience through the lenses of a developmental psychologist, a marxian economist, a freudian analyst, or what predominant perspective? We all have these perspectives; no one comes *tabula rasa* to any human experience and it is healthy to place it on the table. But in addition, this perspective will serve your effort in several ways: (1) it adds intensity, depth and clarity by orienting you and your reader in a common frame of reference, (2) it gives the two of you a refined language-set with which to sensitively describe this human experience. Moreover, (3) it sensitizes you to a variety of concerns and possibilities you would not ordinarily think of as you explore this foreign territory. One danger must be avoided; while a particular perspective can sensitize you, it dare not blind you to the many possibilities of meaning which lie beyond its limited definition of reality. Generally, this encapsulation is best overcome merely by raising its possibility to your conscious awareness.

Comment: Some authors suggest assuming a theoretic neutrality to avoid bias. This is psychologically naive; each of us has a cultural and theoretic orientation that is deeply imbedded in our personality. Not only can it not be put aside like a casual jacket, but it is essential to our ability to understand the world around us. We can declare our orientation but we cannot eliminate it.

Comment: Qualitative research distinguishes between bias and perspective. 'Perspective' acknowledges that the researcher 'sees' the world from a particular vantage point. To the degree that the researcher knows and acknowledges this perspective, it is possessed and controlled,—an essential, powerful tool of the research process. 'Bias,' on the other hand, refers to all that hidden (unconscious) 'ethnocentrism' of the researcher which subtly blinds both researcher and reader to a faithful understanding of the human phenomenon under investigation.

The qualitative researcher minimizes bias, not by placing the research selections beyond choice, posing an innocent neutrality, but by raising these choices up to a level of consciousness, and assuming professional responsibility for their affect on the results.

Selecting Your Subjects and Their Setting. Whether working with documents or in field participation, you are as likely to 'find' the topic of an interesting study by a chance accident as by a well laid plan. One student discovered a set of interview tapes and documents in the Yale Library recording the May Day crisis of 1969 and elected to recreate this dramatic week from the perspective of decision-making theory. Another attended a little people's convention and did participant observation on what happens when three and one-half foot people become the dominant society and six footer's, the deviants. In these two modes, the choice is as often one of responding to a chance opportunity or of adapting to settings as one proceeds as it is to pre-selecting a suitable site for your topic.

In contrast, as an interviewer, you are more likely to pre-select, not only the human experience to be explored, but the specific group through whom it will be discovered. First, set the criteria outlining the particular group you wish to engage. Typically (but not always) your subjects should be people who are reflective and able to verbalize their experiences. Beyond this, select a group that is balanced: not so narrow in their characteristics (age, sex, ethnic, religious, economic status, etc.) that each replicates the other, and not so broad that each becomes a unique case and lacks commonality with the others. To maintain this optimum balance, you will probably modify your pre-selected characteristics as your research proceeds. In all cases, your conscious, careful selection is the correct procedure in contrast to the random, blind strategy of statistical research.

'How many subjects?' is an interesting and frustrating question which can be answered only in the process. One author speaks of the point of ' theoretic saturation,' i.e. that number of interviewees necessary to transcend the unique experiences of each subject and to discover the underlying pattern of human experience shared by all of them. Researchers report an interesting experience over and over again: a period of insight—of recognition of the transcending pattern—and beyond which further interviews produce confirmation and reinforcement, but no new insights.

Actually, the research issue is not numbers—how many?—but depth of involvement. Researchers have been quite successful in discovering a human experience through one person—a case study—and others have briefly interviewed dozens with benefit. However human dynamics being what they are, eight to twelve indepth interviews usually mark a saturation point; beyond this point, extended research tends to move the analysis away from depth toward a numerical-survey modality.

Gatekeeping. Your first step into the field is generically called 'gatekeeping,' and refers to the various protocols and procedures used by the researcher to enter the human setting properly. For the qualitative researcher, the setting is not an impersonal lab, ever waiting for academic attention, but a human setting with an integrity and ethical priority of its own. In fact, the qualitative researcher has been allowed to participate in the most intimate of moments in the lives of respondents. Nevertheless, this has been a sacred trust, freely granted, not a 'right' nor a procedure to be engaged impersonally and without sensitivity. Moreover, personal trust and rapport are essential to a successful research effort and are the goals of the gatekeeping process. This process extends throughout and even beyond the research project itself.

For the participant observer, it begins with the formal and informal requests for admission which must be negotiated at all levels. Even when you have received formal permission 'from above,' you cannot presume or claim it from the responsible person in the immediate area. On the formal levels, offer your credentials indicating the seriousness and 'legitimacy' of your purpose, and explain the purposes of your research and the involvement requested in their setting. While you will probably begin with a letter, a face to face meeting is very desirable and, in itself, will be the beginning of your participant observation research.

An important part of this step is contracting: what you promise them in return for their cooperation with you. This may include promises not to reveal identities, to share or not share results with certain parties, to offer return services, etc. It usually involves written consent forms to both clarify the purpose of your research and to confirm the agreements made.

The participant observer must walk a delicate line between engaging the human environment but not disturbing it. The entry must be gradual, allowing the environment to 'absorb' the researcher without it attributing to him or her a major role that transforms the environment into something different. The researcher must softly 'legitimize' his or her presence to the satisfaction of the new colleagues without becoming an anomaly or a spectacle. The objective is to gain 'insider' rapport, and gradually a participant's understanding of his environment—all without losing researcher objectivity. Even the termination requires a responsible, undisturbing departure that leaves an 'open door' for further query, should it prove necessary.

The interviewer follows a similar but less lengthy procedure. Obtaining interviewees usually succeeds more through personal context and leads to a 'friend of a friend' than through impersonal contacts such as newspaper advertisements. (However, there are no absolutes in qualitative research.) Frequently, you can easily contact several responsive people if you merely share your research interests freely with your friends and colleagues and then request further leads from your initial interviewees.

> *Comment:* Note once again the contrast of the statistical need for an unbiased, random selection of subjects to qualitative's priority for subjects who offer a bond of trust and a willingness to share openly their personal experience of a life situation. This priority leads to different norms for client selection.

Once you have identified some potential subjects, a typical procedure is a personal or telephone contact, followed by a more detailed letter and a follow up call setting the time and place. A letter can also help the interviewee focus on your topic as well as take care of the more depersonalizing paper work—demographics (age, occupation, etc.) and written consent forms. However, your own sense of human relations is your preferred guide to this initial engagement.

Select a setting that is comfortable and supportive to both you and the subject, usually in their environment. If you already have a role relationship with the interviewee, choose a setting (and dress) that will minimize that predisposing relationship.

Interview Techniques. The various methods of interviewing reflect our previous discussion on the emic/etic polarity. Your study may prefer a more structured interview because you are able to assume the major categories or categorical frame of reference of the human experience you wish to study and your interest is to develop more specific, detailed information under these categories. As you estimate the need, you develop a few open ended questions or an entire series of specific questions (there are varying degrees of pre-structure), and present this schedule to each interviewee in the same manner. However, even structured interviews must allow the respondents room to express their thoughts and experiences without being pressed too heavily by your built-in predispositions. Structured interviews are more cognitive and specific, and offer clear, well organized information. Since they are pre-categorized, they are also much easier to analyze.

In the more open-ended, 'emic' interview, usually called 'focussed,' your objective is to capture the subject's total experience, focally and contextually, cognitively and emotionally, with as little intrusion as possible from your frame of reference. Prepare by first developing, in writing, a list of all the 'puzzlements' you hold about the research question. To enhance even greater depth and sensitivity with your interviewee, you should even interview yourself—possibly with the aid of a friend—thereby bringing out for conscious identity all your predispositions on the topic. Then, with all this in mind, prepare a single statement to present to your interviewee which will focus his or her response but predisposes its content and organization as little as possible. For example, "Tell me what is it like to be a step-parent?"

Once this preliminary work is done, meet with the respondent and initiate the interview with this single question. Allow the respondent to share his or her perceptions with as little intrusion or direction and as much verbal and non-verbal encouragement as possible. Encourage the account with rogerian 'yes's' and 'I understand' and 'say more about that' etc. The hoped-for objective is not only an account of the experience, but allowing the respondent to choose all the terms, to arrange the order and hierarchy of ideas, to make the interconnections—etc.—to fully express the experience entirely as he or she perceives it. When the interviewee is 'talked out,' you may then want to follow up with some of the puzzlements not yet addressed, but carefully wording them in the language set and frame of reference of your respondent. Focussed interviews are much less organized and more difficult to analyze, but they are richer in affective quality and take you deeper into this person's understanding of the focal experience.

Recording and Stabilizing Your Data. Recording the material is usually a multiple technique, involving some mechanical instruments (e.g. audio-tape), and some personal note taking by the researcher. The value of tape recorders, by themselves, is over estimated. Our scientifically oriented minds see them as both accurate and objective. In fact, audio-tapes 'select out' a majority of the material—the context, the non-verbal language, the visual response— everything other than the abstracted voice. And obviously, they don't move the data into meaningful form. In contrast, note-taking by the researcher perceives a wide range of data, and, if we trust the self as the primary research instrument, it continually focuses in on the significant and the essential and begins the organizing process of 'making sense.' Moreover, with a little discipline and training, the researcher can develop a fascinating level of memory and accuracy of post-interview notes. The preferred arrangement of most researchers is to combine the two, use a tape recorder during the interview and take detailed notes immediately afterward. This allows the researcher to fully participate in the conversation without fear of losing peripheral material which only a more objective listener would capture.

> *Comment:* Working with the research material plays more than a functional role in the research process. Certainly, it secures the researcher's experience, especially the more ephemeral contextual and affective elements, most of which 'evaporate' the first day. But in addition, working with the data intensifies the researcher's concentration and supports the mind's 'meaning-making,' thinking process. The greater the immersion into the data, the sooner and more faithful the final interpretative theory.

Note taking is frequently a three staged process. The interviewer does not want the engagement distracted by having to take lengthy notes; the participant observer cannot walk around with a pencil and pad in his hand. During the interview or immediately after the participation, jot down pivotal words or topics which note the important items or incidents which occurred, usually in their time sequence. Then make an immediate opportunity to be totally undisturbed and fill in around this skeletal outline all the details you can remember about the engagement. Begin with the informational elements, but build out to include paralingual, non-verbal and contextual elements. Write up as complete and faithful an account as possible. Finally, before twenty-four hours have passed, usually before retiring, return to your notes and annotate them with everything else you have been able to remember about the engagement.

The note taking is a dialogue between two separate forms: (1) descriptive notes recording everything you objectively heard or saw, and (2) interpretive notes of whatever meanings you are developing from this experience. The latter includes both the immediately assumed meanings of interview data, (especially the nonverbal data), and the gradually accumulated collection of hunches interrelating and interpreting the entire experience. Your note-taking will continually move from one form to the other. Initially the interpretive thoughts and hunches will be minimal but then gradually increase. In both areas, writing yourself out is an important part of the research process.

Many authors recommend keeping a third set of methodology or research process notes recording all the significant incidents which occurred and selective choices you made as your research progressed. This latter set of notes will be used in the 'journal' section of the report to be described below.

Next comes the painful choice as to whether to completely transcribe all your tapes (approximately six hour of typing to one hour of recording) or whether to work directly from the tapes and transcribe selectively only the significant quotations, anecdotes and incidents. Some researchers choose to work from complete sets of typewritten notes, analyzing them via a color or numerical code system right on the transcripts themselves; others prefer to break their material down to unit-thoughts of about paragraph size and then place these on separate, codable cards. Once more, your method of managing your data is decided by 'whatever works for you or has been your habit over the years.' The important consideration is to move your material into a stable from which that you find managable.

Comment: Keep in mind that the research process—gathering data, putting it in permanent form, analyzing it, and generating a report—is not a sequential activity, one stage after the other, but an undulating process, continuously swinging back and forth from one activity to the other.

Analysis. Analysis refers both to your on-going task of bringing order to your raw material—discovering its underlying meaning—and to a first stage of the presentation of that material in the report. This latter presentation represents a 'midway' stage on your journey toward understanding of the human experience. Its unique mission is to provide the reader with a first hand involvement with the data itself in the form of quotations and anecdotes, etc., but supports him by carefully selecting this data, structuring it into the researcher's categories and tying it together by the researcher's commentary. It is called 'analysis' because it breaks the experience down into its specific categories and concentrates on the unique properties and characteristics of each category. In the next section, the synthesis, the experience will be presented as a whole. There, these same categories will be assembled together in their interrelationship, revealing 'the whole which is greater than the sum of its parts.'

While your two chapters, analysis and synthesis, will appear quite different, you will arrive at them through the same research process. As you pore over your notes, continually look for units of thought, i.e. organizing ideas around which some of the material can be drawn together and considered as a unit. As you identify these possible organizers, work in two directions. Within the unit of thought, examine your notes and gather together all the material which properly fits under that topical unit. If the material is too substantial, see if it can appropriately be divided into two more manageable units. Once you have identified all the units across your material, begin then to study the material of each, looking for subtopics and identifying the various characteristics or properties which uniquely describe that unit. Organizing it out, attempt to 'tell the story' of that unit-idea, both with your sense of a guiding theme and the resources of your interviewee's significant quotations and symbolic anecdotes.

Move also in the other direction. Identify parallel units until the entire expanse of your material has appropriate unit-designations. It is not necessary to organize all of your material into units, but certainly all the material you consider significant. When all the units are identified, look at them as a set and begin studying their interrelationships,—how are they connected to one another?, which are more focal and which are more supportive background elements?, how in interconnection do they reveal this human experience? Work with your set both to interconnect and 'pattern' the units, and to discover the overarching, unifying thought that pulls these individual units into a single story, a single interpretation. When this 'a ha' of insight emerges from your concentration, you will have arrived at your synthesis or your final interpretation.

During the process, it may happen that you will become unsatisfied with the units you have identified, individually and/or as a set. Your growing familiarity with your material will enable you to conceive of a better set of categories that more appropriately organize and present your material. This is a common and healthy occurrence. Make a fresh copy of your transcribed data and begin anew to sort out and develop this new categorical set. The labor you have lost will be more than compensated for by your greater satisfaction. What you are looking for is a feeling of a 'fit,', an often reported internal feeling of appropriateness. You will 'know' when your concepts are forced and inadequate to the experience, and again feel personally satisfied when the 'right set' emerges in your mind. This phase of the research requires strenuous false starts and extended, patient concentration.

For the final report, the 'analysis' section presents the selected, significant material under the outline of the topical units, usually called 'themes.' Under each theme, the 'story' of each is skillfully told by the researcher but the reader's awareness and involvement is much more on the first hand material—the quotations and anecdotes—than it is on the researcher. When the 'job' is well done, the reader has little awareness of the organizing effort of the researcher; the report seems natural and appropriate—'just the way it is in real life.'

> *Comment:* Abstract titles such as 'methodology,' 'analysis,' etc. are less desirable in qualitative reports. The researcher is encouraged to find a metaphoric set of chapter titles which reflect both the content and mission of each chapter and, at the same time, the overarching interpretation of the study as a whole.

Synthesis. In the analytic section, the data, the experience itself, speaks to the reader, while the researcher and his or her supportive organization stand in the background—much like a guide at a museum. In the synthesis, the researcher moves to the foreground and speaks directly to the reader without the 'show and tell' of the data. In the analysis, the reader focuses in detail on each theme—each piece that makes up the whole. In the synthesis, the reader meets the experience as an integrated whole.

While, to the reader, the two appear strikingly different from each other, the interpretive effort flows smoothly from analysis to synthesis; it is a continuum of the same process. The synthesis is the enveloping interpretive theory which draws together all the thought-units, places them into their unique interrelationship, and unfolds the researcher's understanding of this human experience. Ideally, this interpretation should be both insightful into the human experience and, at the same time, simple and clear. Not only will the reader easily remember the author's interpretation, but he will have identified something of his own human nature in it.

Although the broad spectrum of the synthetic interpretation is rather logical and conceptual in its modality, it achieves a heightened degree of unity and memorability by being 'clothed' and illustrated by a metaphor—a picturesque illusion which both characterizes and further integrates in image form the heart of the interpretation. Such images have the power of resonating with layers of personal experiences of the reader. For these very reason, Freud and many others have utilized Greek mythological figures to synthesize much of their insights. Fairy tales are also rich sources: e.g. the Cinderella syndrome, the Peter Pan complex, etc. Single words reflecting ordinary daily experiences are often adequate. Some researchers have used drama, liturgy, dance, games and other common 'metaphoric' experiences from everyday life as the organizers and interpreting devices for their theory.

Commentary. Having now completed your task of bringing understanding to this human experience, you have now earned your right to comment with authority in this final section of your research report. And your commentary may extend in various directions. You may now wish to respond to the literature of others who have presented research in this same theoretic area, comparing or contrasting their findings with yours, commenting or expanding upon their theory, etc. You may wish to draw various implications on how your discovery can affect present professional practice or how its insights might be integrated into present theory. Or you might choose to suggest further research that could contribute significantly to the theoretic base of this human experience. One or two of these commentaries, clearly developed because they have already compelled you may well be presented. Presenting several commentaries, especially in response to the ritual of reports, should be avoided.

Methodological Journal. Frequently an account of the researcher's process is attached as an epilogue to published pieces of qualitative research. In a dissertation, it becomes the 'methodology' chapter, but has a genre unique to the qualitative approach. Rather than an idealized plan or a detailed recipe for replication, its style is that of a personal account, a disclosive journal of the initial best laid plan and the unexpected events, turns and choices and even pitfalls that lead to the final results. Here are disclosed the perspectives and values of the researcher as they influenced the research engagement. Usually the account is organized around a theme—such as his movement from being a total outsider to gaining insider acceptance. Interestingly enough, this unpretentious disclosure of how the project was 'really researched' is qualitative's method of allowing the reader to evaluate the credibility of the research presentation.

Final Report. The draft of your research report 'emerges' from your accumulating descriptive and interpretive notes developed throughout your study. You have been writing it since you first attempted to articulate your focal question. As noted above, you write with as much precision and sensitivity as you can, you leave your writing to re-experience your field, and then you return and rewrite once more, each time more faithfully articulating the experience you are focusing on. The field you engage is as much the author of your report as you are.

When you have developed a 'good' draft, your role as 'student' of the experience comes to an end and you shift your role to that of 'educator' with the task of communicating your experience to your reader. In this role, you not only want to 'tell' your reader what you, the researcher, have come to understand, but more, you want to recreate, in a facilitated form, the experience of the discovery itself.

Rewrite your material so that the movement from the title and initial focal question, through the unfolding of units of thought, to final interpretive understanding is smoothly and economically communicated to the reader. Ideally, your reader 'discovers' your interpretive insight without ever feeling lost, wading through unorganized data, or manipulated, pressured into your conclusions. The reader's consciousness should be entirely immersed in the 'real' and 'alive' experience you are sharing; there should be little consciousness that it is a research report that is being read. And in the end, the reader should have acquired your insight into the experience as if it were his or her own. This is the objective of your final rewrite.

The task may sound near impossible but there are hundreds of others who have successfully proceeded you. Don't hesitate to have an outside reader give you feedback as you make your final draft. Few qualitative researchers claim to be natural, professional writers, but if your study is alive in you, and if you now refocus your attention to your reader and the reader's process of understanding, the task will be both manageable and successful. If there is one testimonial which characterizes the final estimate of qualitative researchers, it is that the path was hard but it was also exciting and engaging to the very end.

Selected Bibliography

Comments: The following are a few of the more popular 'methods' books in qualitative research. The reader will find them more serviceable by moving directly to the section reflecting his immediate needs (e.g. 'interviewing') rather than digesting entire books. Note that each book, as this article, represents one author's research strategy; there are no established, prescribed procedures, only the norm of clear and credible results.

Barzun, J., and Graff, H. F. (1977). *The modern researcher* (3rd. ed.). New York: Harcourt Brace Jovanovich, Inc.

Bogdan, R. and Bicklen, S. (1982). *Qualitative research for education: An introduction to theory and methods.* Boston: Allyn and Bacon, Inc.

Glaser, B. G. and Strauss, A. L. (1967). *The discovery of grounded theory.* Chicago: Aldine Publishing Co.

Goetz, J. P. and LeCompte, M. D. (1984). *Ethnography and qualitative design in educational research.* Orlando, FL: Academic Press.

Johnson, J. M. (1975). *Doing field research.* New York: The Free Press.

Lofland, J. (1971). *Analyzing social settings: A guide to qualitative observation and analysis.* Belmont, CA: Wadsworth Publishing Co.

Patton, M. (1980). *Qualitative evaluation methods.* Beverly Hills, CA: Sage Sage Publications.

Schatzman, L. and Strauss, A. L. (1973). *Field research: Strategies for a natural sociology.* Englewood Cliffs, NJ: Prentice-Hall.

Sjoberg, G. and Nett, R. (1968). *A methodology for social research.* New York: Harper and Row.

Spradley, J. P. (1979). *The ethnographic interview.* New York: Holt Rinehart and Winston.

Taylor, S. J. and Bogdan, R: (1984). *Introduction to qualitative research methods: The search for meanings.* New York: John Wiley & Sons.

Chapter Six
The Role of the Statistical Consultant
Michael W. Hurst, Ed.D

Introduction

Before I discuss the role of the statistical consultant it is worthwhile for you to understand the perspective from which I am coming in writing this Chapter. I was granted my doctorate degree in January 1974 after completing the requirements which included a doctorate dissertation in September 1973.

I later served on six dissertation committees and eventually evolved a consulting practice that included a lot of consulting to dissertation candidates and their committees. The dissertations came from schools granting the Ph.D., Ed.D, and Psy.D. degrees. These colleges and universities included Boston University, Harvard College, Radcliffe College, Northeastern University, Boston College, University of Michigan, University of Virginia, Florida State University, Pacific Western University, University of California, Oklahoma State University and even the University of Glascow (Scotland).

By way of my own experience and the experience of assisting others in this process as a statistical consultant, I was exposed to a number of different philosophies and perspectives regarding the quality, style and politics of doctorate dissertations and the committees which supervised their completion. If there is one important thing that you can gather from all of this experience, it would be to remember that your committee is the responsible party for the final disposition of your dissertation and that you are the final authority on what you accomplished. A consultant, whether statistical or otherwise, can only advise you, broaden your perspective, suggest alternative ways of doing things, and perhaps even help you conduct some of the mechanical operations such as statistical analysis. However, the final arbiter of whether or not your work is good is your committee and perhaps eventually the scientific press if you attempt to get your dissertation findings published.

What Is a Statistical Consultant?

A statistical consultant is basically a person who has greater training (but not necessarily a specific degree) and experience in research design, statistical analysis, table presentation design, figure design, and technical writing skills than your own. The consultant should have a mastery of non-parametric and parametric statistical tests and certainly should know statistics through the multivariate level. The consultant should be familiar with the variety of post-hoc multiple comparison statistics such as Scheffe's, Tukey, Duncan's and so on. The person hopefully has experience dealing with categorical, discontinuous, biological, and psychometric types of data. These types of data have different naturally occurring distributions and don't all necessarily yield themselves to nice, neat "normal" distributions. Perhaps most importantly the statistical consultant should know the underlying assumptions used for deriving and calculating the various statistics and their implications for your particular analyses and types of data.

Hopefully the statistical consultant is a person who has an "objective" point of view. The consultant shouldn't care which way answers go in "proving" or "disproving" your hypothesis. By way of contrast your committee members have a vested interest in the outcome of your research since they approved it as worthwhile and worth testing. As for yourself, you have a vested bias in having the results appear in the same direction as your "expected findings". Of the 100 or so dissertations to which I was a consultant, only 10–20% had results that were in support of the expected findings. So you should not be disappointed if your results do not come out as you had anticipated. The potential influences on your data and analyses are enumerable and cannot all be anticipated.

Only those projects which build upon a long and well established line of research and extend only a single particular area for that line of research have a high probability of achieving the anticipated findings. But even in that limited case, there very often are surprises. Hopefully, you can maintain an open attitude towards your data and findings because sometimes the most important findings are totally unanticipated.

The statistical consultant is also a person who will help interpret the numbers you generate in your analyses and should be interested and capable of making suggestions for alternative analyses. In so doing the consultant can help anticipate the kinds of questions and suggestions that your committee members may make. Thereby you will have done a more complete job before presenting even preliminary findings to your committee.

The statistical consultant's real role should be as your tutor in understanding the statistical and analytical process involved in your dissertation and should act as a second opinion on committee suggestions but not as a substitute member of your committee. Remember the committee always has the last word.

Hopefully the statistical consultant also will be a person who can empathize with the dissertation process. Even the most confident, competent person with whom I consulted had periods of great frustration, anxiety, anger, marital conflict, job conflict and so forth arise as a consequence of this process which often extends over many months and sometimes years. The statistical consultant is not simply a computer or a statistical dictionary but needs to help you get through those periods and deal with those issues that interfere with the completion of the process.

Finally the statistical consultant should help you interpret and clarify committee politics. Occasionally the consultant may interface with committee members to understand the intent of their instructions and suggestions. This area of interpretation and clarifying of committee politics is, perhaps, one that will surprise you, but the politics of power exists on dissertation committees as they do in any joint human endeavor. Sometimes you will find yourself having to do analyses that will make no sense whatsoever to you or your consultant, but you should do them anyhow to satisfy the needs of committee members who wish to demonstrate either their expertise or thoroughness in considering your project. On the other hand, some committee members will have very few things to say about the statistics and analysis used in your study but may have their own hypothesis or alternative explanations that they would like you to pursue. You will need to work very carefully with your committee chairperson to try to understand both the intent and necessity of the various viewpoints that will be presented on the committee and how you might best cope with them.

Your consultant should help in this political process. Such help is really needed when the chairperson is presenting you with a difficult position in spite of the fact that he/she is your main sponsor. The consultant can act as your coach in presenting results to the committee. The consultant can help you consider the different motivations, investments, and interests that are represented by the committees' questions and suggestions.

Do You Need a Statistical Consultant?

This question is extraordinarily difficult to answer because there are at least five areas which you must consider.

First do you have the training and experience to comfortable and confidently design your research, conduct your research, analyze the results, pursue the alternatives and present the findings to your particular committee? Sometimes individuals have managed to pull together a committee that is very tough and rigorous in these areas to the extent that the candidate, though having had the necessary course work and some experience, feels unsure and intimidated. A consultant sometimes can simply help to restore your confidence in your abilities.

However, sometimes the training and the experience you had is basically insufficient to pursue your particular research design and statistical analysis. In this case you really might want to consider a consultant or, as I discuss shortly, using a statistical specialist on your committee.

There are some other aspects to the training and experience question. Many people, especially in the helping professions, have what amounts to a number phobia. That is, they have a basic anxiety in dealing with quantifiable concepts

65

and conducting mathematical computations. Sometimes these people pursue the route of a non-numerical, non-analytical dissertation which is a fine solution if one's college or committee will allow it. In other cases a research and statistical consultant can help overcome the phobia in a functional sense.

Another related "phobia" is with respect to computers. Computers are advantageous for all the number "crunching" in dissertation projects even if the data base is quite small. The primary advantage is that the calculations have already been programmed and they will come out correct as long as the data input has been done correctly. You can try many different analyses without having to spend hours at a calculator with a paper and pencil. Generally there is far less probability of errors in the computational process itself. So if you have the fear of computers, a consultant can help in this area because the consultant inevitably will use computers in assisting you with your analyses.

Secondly, you can consider whether or not you already have or can choose either a chairperson or other committee member who is a statistical specialist. Some colleges or departments have the requirement that a statistically expert individual be a member of every dissertation committee, but this requirement is not always the case. If it is the case in your particular school, you hopefully will choose or ask a statistical specialist who has some of the more empathic perspectives that I suggested a consultant should have and that person thereby may be an internal consultant for you. If your department does not have this requirement or you do not have an available person, then you may have little choice but to find a statistical consultant who can help you in the ways that I have already indicated.

Thirdly, you need to consider how you use your time if you are weak in research design, statistical analysis, use of the computer, or interpreting numbers. If you don't use a consultant, you are going to spend a lot of time just learning what to do and making a very large number of mistakes. Using a consultant obviously can cut down the actual time needed to accomplish the particular analyses and interpretations. You thereby will have more time to spend on understanding your results and presenting them in a viable form.

Time also may be a consideration if, as many dissertation candidates, you have other commitments for your time. Many people to whom I consulted had a job in addition to their educational responsibility. They took perhaps a year at squeezing out precious time from family, home, or social life to conduct the research and had little time to do the "number crunching" for example. Using a statistical consultant was a viable alternative for them to cope with these other commitments.

On the other hand, many dissertation candidates don't have another job or other significant commitment and may have the time to go through the learning process to accomplish their project on their own. The issue of time is one that only you can solve—as are most of the others that I raise with respect to using a statistical consultant.

Fourthly, you need to consider the issue of money. A statistical consultant generally will have to be hired unless your university or department has an internal statistical consulting unit that is free for everybody to use. Unless such a unit is available to you, you'll have to think about whether you can afford an outside consultant. The question will be resolved in part as you talk to potential consultants and ask how much they charge. Very often the charges can be minimal if the individual does it as a sideline to their main career work. Other times the charges can be a significant expense if consulting is the main line of work that the potential consultant pursues.

The major difference between using an internal and external consultant is somewhat dependent on who will give you the most concentrated and focussed work on your behalf. Internal statistical units often have dozens of people they are assisting whereas the external consultant often has only a few—which consulting load has an impact on both their price and how much time they can dedicate to your particular project. Again this is an issue that you will have to solve and you will have to qualify your internal and external consultant candidates along this line.

Fifthly, you need to consider the issue of whether you have the connections within your university or department that give you access to the necessary computer equipment, software, and data entry services that will be needed. A statistical consultant will have all of this available within his or her practice, but even if they don't, they surely will have made it available to themselves through some other connections outside of their practice. Internal statistical consultants also will have had or will have made the necessary connections with the computer department to accomplish projects such as yours. My observation is that many universities provide "free" computer time, software packages, and data preparation services for their students and especially for their doctoral students. It is very worthwhile to take seminars or other course offerings by the computer department in order to familiarize yourself with these "free" services, but in particular, to meet people who make services available and who can make your use of the services either easy or difficult for you. If you don't do this and you decide not to have a consultant, you will find these "connection" aspects as being some of the most frustrating of the whole process.

When Should I Get a Consultant?

Assuming that you are going to use a consultant—whether internal or external, the best advice is that you should have that person involved in your dissertation process as soon as possible. Some university departments and some committees require a prospectus which is a statement of your problem, a review of research, and suggested hypotheses to be investigated. Others require that the prospectus include your research design and suggested statistical analyses. Obviously if your committee or department is one of the former, then

67

you involve the consultant at the time that your prospectus has been accepted for investigation as your dissertation. In the latter case you may want to have a consultant involved as you begin considering how you are to design an appropriate research paradigm and what statistical analysis may be used with it. Basically you may wish to engage a consultant as soon as you are considering the issue of how you are going to answer your research questions in terms of design and/or analysis.

I have been in the unfortunate position of having been asked in at a stage when an individual may have failed their final oral hearing and/or have the final written draft rejected for reasons of incomplete, inadequate, or inappropriate design and analysis. You do not want to wait until this happens! I am not suggesting that it will happen to you, but very often you won't know until it is too late for you and a great deal of re-working may have to be accomplished.

You also may wish to consider that the later you bring in a consultant, the more you are going to have to pay that consultant just to educate that person with respect to what you have done and for what reasons. You also may find that at a later stage the consultant may have many valuable suggestions for you to consider and even may have some major criticisms. The suggestions and criticisms probably will be directed at how you conducted your study and what the results imply for your hypotheses. Thus, just as you wish to have your committee members involved in the process all the way along, you should have your consultant, if you use one, involved as early as possible.

How to Find a Statistical Consultant

Once you have determined that you would like to use a statistical consultant, you can find one in several places. In the course of deciding whether or not you wanted one, you undoubtedly talked to faculty members and prior dissertation candidates. The faculty and the prior dissertation candidates are the best sources of reliable and helpful statistical consultants in the dissertation process. You should try to get at least two names so that you can have a choice and not feel totally locked into someone you may not like in terms of style, personality, or orientation.

After you have some names of consultants, you should give your potential consultants a call. In this first contact you let them know how you got their name, who recommended them, your timetable for accomplishing your study and what the basic outline of what you see as your biggest need for help. You should ask whether or not all of these seem reasonable to the person and what they have for available time and what they charge. You also would be interested in what resources they have to help you in the process.

If you find that you don't personally like the potential consultant or if some of the parameters about which you inquired were unsatisfactory for your particular circumstance, you should ask the consultant for another referral.

Undoubtedly the consultant will know other individuals who do similar things. You then would call these referrals and present the same questions and issues you asked of your initial referrals.

In the event that you can not come up with any referrals from faculty, prior dissertation candidates, or even other consultants, there are several other sources that you should consider. The mathematics departments of most universities have a statistical section and very often that section provides statistical consultation to students and other faculty in the university. Very often the consultants will be senior graduate students and will have a very mathematical and precise focus. However, they can provide you some of the best technically accurate information and consulting and very often for no or a small fee.

The second most likely source of a statistical consultant for your dissertation is the computer department at the university. By computer department I mean both the academic computer department and the computer center staff. In either location you may find individuals who have done a lot of consulting, either formally or informally, for a fee or for free depending on university policy. These people will have much less of a statistical research focus and much more of a focus on getting your particular statistics computed. These people also are most helpful in helping you set up your data acquisition forms such that data entry is easy. They also are quite helpful in terms of formatting results so that they are more easily comprehended once all of the numbers are cranked out by the computer. You also may find on the bulletin board of the computer center free-lance consultants who will help with statistical processing, but these individuals will tend to be students who are doing it for a few spare dollars. Although some of them may be very good, their reliability sometimes will be very poor due to their own needs.

Finally, there are commercial data processing services that are listed in the telephone book under data processing. These services either have on-staff people who are capable of helping directly for the usual charge of the business or they know of people that they or their clients use for those purposes. This route is probably the most expensive. You must be very clear about the conditions of your contract such that you do not run up tremendous data entry, processing, or other bills. Hence, if you use a commercial service, be very explicit as to what your budget is and be as explicit as possible about what your actual statistical needs are so that too many analyses are not run.

Thus finding a competent statistical consultant is similar to finding any other service provider. Just as references and prior satisfied users are the best evaluators of a health care provider, such persons are the best contacts for a statistical consultant.

If you can locate committee members and prior dissertation candidates who have used a potential consultant, you can find out how that consultant interacted with the individual as well as with the committee. You should determine whether or not the suggestions and alternatives proposed by the consultant were received well or not. Again, remember that your dissertation committee is the most important evaluator of your work and thereby of the work of the consultant whom you choose. It is important that the consultant understand the committee in terms of the particular department or the university, or, even better, in terms of the particular individuals on that committee. This understanding will minimize false starts and inappropriate analyses.

How to Qualify Your Statistical Consultant

Although I raised some basic questions that you should ask in initially calling a consultant, you still may not wish to use that particular consultant after you have had a face-to-face meeting. You should use the telephone call simply to screen the potential consultant on practical matters. The next stage of qualifying the consultant is somewhat more sophisticated.

You probably will be interested in the nature and quality of the relationship you form with that consultant. There is no particular relationship that is good for everybody. You need to evaluate how well you get along with the consultant in talking to him or her in the face-to-face situation. After all, you will be relating to that person for a number of hours over the course of months and years and the two of you should be able to get along. If you can't, you can just say that the match is not quite right and ask for another potential consultant.

You will want to examine the communication skills of your consultant both in written and verbal forms. The consultant should be able to provide you with copies of research articles or other articles he or she may have written. You should be able to comprehend their writing. If you have a consultant who writes in a very technical and difficult-to-understand style, then the person probably will influence you into a similar style. Therefore, take a look at the written style that the consultant has used in the past.

In terms of verbal abilities, you have to judge those directly in terms of how well, how clearly, and how concisely the consultant describes the issues in your study. These judgements lead to another area of qualifying your consultant.

The verbal qualifications are judged best from the consultant's responses to your study description. The potential consultant should be able to describe the strengths and weaknesses of your study in a clear and succinct way. Even though you already (hopefully) know these strengths and weaknesses, the consultant very definitely should know them, and in addition, will or should be able to raise new strengths and weaknesses in a comprehensible fashion. The consultant should be able to raise issues and questions that you need to resolve yourself and/or with your committee in terms of the design and conduct of your study. The consultant should be able to describe methods by which you may be able to resolve those issues in question. Basically, you are looking for someone who is reasonably good at communicating with you in a understandable way. It makes no difference whether or not anybody else can communicate with the consultant because you are going to be the one talking to him/her. If you can paraphrase and clearly describe your understanding and your paraphrasing is a match with the consultant's understanding, then you can be reasonably confident that the two of you are communicating well enough for productive work.

If your consultant was not referred by faculty or prior candidates who worked with or used a consultant, you should ask for some references that you can call. You also should be very careful to outline your general schedule for accomplishing your dissertation. The consultant should be able to meet that schedule in terms of its feasibility and in terms of the consultant's time availability to assist you. The consultant should be able to give you estimated response times for when you provide data to when the analyses come back to when you get to discuss them. And clearly, the issue of cost should be annunciated and if you simply cannot afford a person, so be it! Ask for somebody who might be less expensive. On the other hand, if you find somebody that qualifies all the way down the line and you communicate with him well and you comprehend your design and statistics better, then it may be worth your while to sacrifice in order to use that particular consultant. The issue of communication is crucial in the statistical area since it is the area that generates a lot of technical misunderstanding as well as fears that need to be resolved. If you and your potential consultant cannot do this well, then you are going to have a very tenuous consulting relationship.

I have outlined in these five sections what I believe are the major issues you face in using a statistical consultant. I may have been too brief, but my comments represent the best distillation of my experience as both a consumer of statistical consultants and as having been a statistical consultant on a wide variety of projects with a wide variety of people at a wide variety of universities.

Chapter Seven

Developmental Difficulties in Dissertating: Intrapsychic and Interpersonal Dilemmas

Edward A. Hattauer, Ph.D. and Steven N. Broder, Ph.D.

The act of "dissertating" is not only an educational odyssey but also a personal pilgrimage. A colleague has compared it to the heroic journey in the *Lord of the Rings* (Tolkien, 1973) one seeks the power of the ring (the doctoral diploma) and along the way there are goblins and witches that hinder one's progress as well as beneficent magicians who aid along the way.

While the inevitable educational bureaucracy places external obstacles in one's path, often the most significant difficulties are posed by the student's internal demons and conflicts that are potentiated by the process. Assuming rigorous selection criteria, almost every doctoral candidate possesses the requisite academic skills to complete the dissertation satisfactorily. Those who do not seem to be stymied largely by their inability to cope with the personal developmental tasks and interpersonal relationships that need to be negotiated in the process.

This chapter delineates three aspects of the intrapsychic and interpersonal process of "dissertating." The first, the developmental task of individuation and separation, suggests the dependency conflicts inherent in the process. Secondly, Bowlby's (1979) concept of a "secure base" is utilized as a model for understanding the importance of the dissertation advisor, as affected by early relationships with attachment figures. Finally, the relationship between the advisee and the advisor as crucial to the former's success is discussed.

Individuation and Separation

Formal education in many respects is a regressive experience as it encapsulates individuals in the safety of its protective womb. For the younger student who has gone directly from undergraduate to graduate work, it sometimes seems that adulthood and emancipation may never result. For the older student who, after life and work experience, has returned to school, graduate work often poses a counterpoint to other roles and tasks. While these students may be full-time workers, spouses, parents, and "established" adults, in graduate school they find themselves once again returned to the status of dependent adolescents.

Often students seem to experience a fluctuation between a devaluation of the entire graduate school process coupled with personal omnipotence: "This is worthless or irrelevant—I know all this." The competing theme is one of self-denigration and overevaluation of the process. "I'll never be as good as Professor Smith and know all that he does." An associated myth is the "Fallacy of the Perfect Dissertation": in order for me to graduate (and separate) I must produce the perfect piece of research.

I (SNB) recall such an individuation and separation crisis at the end of my graduate work. After submitting a revision of my dissertation I received a call from my advisor informing me that the dissertation appeared to be completed and that I should schedule a time for the oral defense with my committee. Initially, the call was met with the joy that accompanies the successful resolution of any long struggle. However, I remember vividly how these feelings were soon replaced by a wave of self-doubt and even fear, "I don't know enough yet. I'm not ready." After these feelings subsided, I realized that with the acceptance of my dissertation, I would now be, at least in an academic and professional sense, a "grown-up."

The Advisor-Advisee Relationship: The Concept of a "Secure Base"

John Bowlby (1979) has written cogently of the importance of an "attachment figure" or "secure base" in fostering the talent and abilities of individuals. Attachment figures are adequate to the extent to which they provide a secure base while at the same time encourage the person to go out and explore. While such a trustworthy, supportive figure is exemplified most often by the parent of young children, Bowlby has argued that having such a secure base is an important requirement for mature adults as well. Indeed different kinds of secure bases are necessary at different phases of the life cycle.

How does a student find an advisor who will be a "secure base"? The application of Bowlby's (1979) construct to the advisory relationship suggests that it is necessary for doctoral candidates to accomplish two sets of tasks. They first must be able to recognize and select an advisor who will provide such a trustworthy base; and secondly, they must have the skills to collaborate with that advisor in such a way that a mutually beneficial relationship is initiated and maintained.

How do problems occur? Bowlby (1979) has pointed out that childhood patterns of interaction with early attachment figures, usually parents, tend to persist and affect both the choice of the figure and the nature of their collaborative interactions. The way in which the student interacts with the emotion-laden figure of the advisor may be affected and perhaps even distorted by the experiences the student had with his parents during his childhood. Advisors, of course, bring their own history of familial baggage that may create problems. It is a very difficult task to attempt to provide sufficient support and direction while at the same time not usurping the autonomy of the student.

Bowlby (1979) uses a cognitive framework and suggests that we each evolve working models of attachment figures who may be conceived as accessible and reliable or a model in which the attachment figure is perceived as being unwilling to respond or responding in a hostile fashion. Similarly, we evolve working models of the self toward whom others will respond in certain predictable ways. When problems arise in the working relationship between advisor and advisee, it may be helpful for both parties to reflect on their current patterns of interaction in an attempt to disentangle unrealistic expectations, perceptions, and miscommunications.

The Advisor as Mentor

When the chicks of a hen are young, she gathers them to her;
when they are grown, she drives them away
—from the rabbinic commentary on Leviticus

Forming a relationship with a mentor is a key developmental task of early adulthood (Levinson, Darrow, Klein, & McKee, 1978). While it is possible to have a mentor who is not a dissertation advisor, it seems that often the mentor and the advisor are the same individual to assume the mantle of mentor. Levinson et al. (1978) state,

The true mentor, in the meaning intended here, serves as an analogue in adulthood of the 'good enough' parent for the child. He fosters the young adult's development by believing in him, sharing the youthful Dream and giving it his blessing, helping to define the newly emerging self in its discovered world, and creating a space in which the young man can work on a reasonable satisfactory life structure that contains the Dream. (pp. 98–99)

Most striking in my (EAH) own dissertation experience was my advisor stating to me that I had different alternatives to consider—options that would result in very different research enterprises. He suggested that I not decide immediately but "live with" the possibilities for a few days. My mentor, thus, allowed and encouraged my own self determination in communicating to me his trust in my ability to make a good choice while also reaffirming his availability if I should need him.

However, problems may arise if the sponsor-mentor fails to encourage the advisee's separation and individuation. Levinson et al. (1978) suggest that the relationship between the sponsor and the advisee is a highly volatile one, not unlike many love relationships. In fact, most of these relationships are said to end with both parties feeling aggrieved: the advisee feels frustrated and resentful that the advisor's approval is gained only by following closely in the latter's footstep, at the expense of breaking new ground; the mentor sees the advisee as overly sensitive and ungrateful.

Broder (1984) has suggested another dynamic which is relevant here. The advisor is continually faced with a "loving and leaving dilemma" in which graduating students with whom there have been a close and productive relationships are experienced as significant losses. Most of the time, pride in the advisee's accomplishments as well as a sense of having passed on something valuable are utilized by advisors to cope with these losses. However, some advisors have great difficulty with the loss of their doctoral students. In such instances, we often see advisees who work diligently, yet do not get their proposals accepted or who are given more books to read each time they bring in a "final revision" of a dissertation chapter.

This chapter has described how the completion of the doctoral dissertation requires much more from the student than intellectual abilities alone. We have proposed the metaphor of a heroic journey, with its arduous tasks which must be endured to obtain the same prized possession. As is often the case, however, it is the journey itself and the personal transformation it produces which becomes valued at the end, even over the prize itself. For the graduate student in the process of dissertating, this transformation is reached only by learning to separate and individuate so that one comes to trust one's own judgment and abilities; and by engaging fully in a productive relationship with one's own advisor who becomes one's colleague.

References

Bowlby, J. (1979). *The making and breaking of affectional bonds*. London: Tavistock Publications.

Broder, S. N. (1984). *The "loving and leaving dilemma": Implications for supervisors and supervisees*. Unpublished manuscript, Boston University.

Levinson, D. J., Darrow, C. N., Klein, E. B., & Levinson, M. H. (1978). *The seasons of a man's life*. New York: Ballantine Books.

Tolkien, J. R. R. (1973). *The lord of the rings*. New York: Ballantine Books.

Chapter Eight
The Final Dissertation
Eileen T. Nickerson, Ph.D.

Rewriting Chapters I, II, and III

If all has gone reasonably well and the original proposal consisting of Chapters I, II, and III were well written, all that is needed for the final dissertation is to change the tenses of these first three chapters from present or future to the past. How simple! So you see all that committee input served more of a purpose than to produce a successful dissertation proposal. It put you in position to concentrate your energies on the final chapter writing; as well as enabling you to conduct a meritorious study.

If however, you had to change procedures or to add some aspects to the study, you will need to rewrite those parts of these chapters to conform to what you actually did, unless you wisely did that as you went along. Occasionally also, some significant piece of research or treatise of your topic has been published since you completed your review of the literature. In these eventualities, these newer materials will need to be integrated with your review. Also obviously if you have done some significant reformulation of any part of the original proposal, this will be added. But for the most part, the first three chapters were put in nearly final form for the original dissertation proposal and all that is needed is a tense change.

Chapter IV—The Results

As some of our popular TV 'cops and robbers' shows note, all we want here are the FACTS and nothing but the facts. Save all your interpretations and explanations of why you found what you found for Chapter Five.

Organization of Chapter Four. Presentation of Hypotheses. Ordinarily you would start off by restating your experimental hypotheses one by one. After each hypotheses, you provide the data in tabular form which indicates whether the hypotheses were rejected or accepted as well as the probability level; and you indicate this in literary form after the statement of the hypotheses. The tabular data is inserted in the most appropriate place after the restatement of the hypotheses and it is referred to in the text describing the status of these hypotheses. Tables are numbered consecutively in dissertations with the first Table becoming number one, no matter where it appears and so on. Do not interpret the meaning of your data as you present it, leave that task for Chapter V.

Now for a word about Tables. As noted previously (Chapter Three), it is expected that you will have surveyed the American Psychological Associations' *Publication Manual* (1983) or the Turabian Manual, if you are using that, before you began your proposal writing. As you will note in these manuals, the general principle of Table or Figure presentation is that each presentation of data be able to 'stand alone', so to speak. That is, tables, graphs, figures, etc., should be sufficiently captioned that they can be understood without reading the entire chapter. The usual error is insufficient and unclear captioning of tables.

Additional Data Analysis. After the presentation of the data either supporting or rejecting your hypotheses, next provide all of the additional data in text and tabular form. These additional analysis include any data which did not involve the direct testing of the hypotheses. Thus, we will find here Descriptive Data regarding your sample, instruments, etc., as well as any additional intercorrelational, analysis of variance and/or factor analyses which you have conducted. If there is a massive amount of tabular data, it is permissable in the interest of clarity to refer to it in the text of Chapter Four, but to remove this data to the Appendices.

Thematic Data and Case Studies. As noted in the chapter on Qualitative Research Design, most of the data to be reported may be in the form of, for example, thematic analyses and case studies. However, this type of material may also appear with dissertations of an experimental or quasi-experimental nature along with the usual testing of hypotheses.

One of the possible modes of handling this type of data is to provide separate chapters for it. For example, prototypes in the form of case studies might be employed to illustrate some feature of the study such as the typical client who profits from the proposed intervention and one who does not; the androgynous and the non-androgynous male college sophomore, etc. You will confer with your advisor, members of the committee and your research consultant in reaching decisions as to how best to present the rich data emanating from the more qualitative and explorative procedures employed in your study.

Summary (of Chapter Four). This section becomes the next to the last of your summaries. Sometimes it is helpful to make a table which summarizes hypotheses tested, the significance level, and statements of rejection or acceptance. This is a particularly helpful procedure if you have tested a number of hypotheses. In any event, give your reader a brief overview of the major findings—and as always the facts, just the facts!

Chapter V—Discussion of the Results

Chapter V is probably the most difficult chapter to write and its best to expect that it usually takes several or more re-write(s) to come sufficiently close to the mark to have it accepted. It is a crucial chapter for it is where you will bring everything together—your expectations for your study, the data actually collected, and the findings and their relevance to the larger body of scholarship in the field, etc. It is your chance to recover and rekindle the original enthusiasm you had for the study and it should be a powerful and compelling chapter. All too often though it reads as though you have "run out of steam" (not to mention ideas and words!).

One of the useful suggestions for writing Chapter V is to lay Chapter IV (Results) aside for awhile after you write it. Then go back and re-read it; do the required revisions of the first three chapters and try to recapture what you were originally trying to do, to understand, to investigate. Then marshal your thoughts for this Chapter (V) into the following sections:

Overview of the Study
Overview of the Results
Implications of the Results in terms of
    Theory
    Research
    Practice
Summary (of the entire study and chapter)

Overview of the Study. Writing the major overview of your study is a difficult job because usually you are so loaded with information, tables, data, and interpretations that you find narrowing yourself down to a few words almost impossible. However, see if in a few pages you can bring your reader from the beginning to the end of your contribution to your field of study. It is perfectly permissible to go back and lift sentences and paragraphs from summaries in the body of your report. Furthermore, if this section is carefully enough written it can be adapted easily for the abstract of your study.

Overview of the Results. In general, a listing of the findings by number, blocked and indented, helps the reader to form a visual gestalt of your work. Here is your chance to integrate the findings of your study with the theory and research that you referred to previously. You ideally should come to some conclusions and not merely raise questions about what you have done. This is particularly true if you have positive findings in your study. It is perfectly permissible in the discussion section of your thesis to quote others' findings and to raise some general doubts about the previous research if yours is in contradiction to what others have found, and/or to point out where your findings support others when they do. In general, you will place your findings within the context of previous scholarly efforts.

Implications of the Results for Theory, Research and Practice. In these sections you will share with your reader all of your dearly earned accumulated wisdom in the general areas of theory, research and practice. Here is your chance to share with enthusiasm your ideas about 'where to from here' with your readers.

For example, in the section on Implications for Research you should share all those gems of research ideas you had but couldn't carry out within the scope of your study. Discuss what you particularly think could and/or should be done in future research. Let your reader benefit from your acquired research expertise. Also, allow your creative tendencies full reign, as you speculate on what your findings say to other scholars and practitioners. Let them know the importance of your study for their work. Delineate any changes in theoretical conceptualizations and pragmatic applications which your findings dictate. Others in the field will ultimately benefit from your considered guidance, as well as from your data.

Summary (of Chapter V). Finally, you come to the last summarizing overview of your study (Hallelujah!). In fact, it may serve as the model (though not exact replica) of the three hundred and fifty word Abstract which you will evolve. Since you have been systematically summarizing your chapters as you went along; and since you have provided a succinct and well integrated overview of your study and its results at the beginning of this chapter; the task of this last synthesizing piece of writing, while formidable enough, is definitely do-able. So go to it with zest and fervor and try to leave your reader on a significant and upbeat note.

The Final Orals

This is it—the 'big time'! As usual the question arises as to how to decide when you are ready for it—your final presentation of your magnus opus and defense of it. Needless probably to say, your advisor and you may decide when its time to set up this final meeting. It ideally comes after your advisor has approved all your chapters, which may prove to be more time-consuming than anticipated, particularly with the last chapter.

At this point you should refer to Chapter Three where detailed considerations involved in preparing and typing the dissertation manuscript are contained. After the required number of copies are made you should disperse these copies to your committee at least two weeks before the final oral. Some members may require more than two weeks and you need to be considerate of the pressures they are under. As a courtesy to your committee, place the copies in black dissertation binders. The copies for the library, however, may be placed in manila folders.

A classic problem is to try to arrange the Final Orals before all the chapters are satisfactorily written. The usual reason for such a development is the desire to graduate by a certain date when all the relatives are planning to be there, etc. All will go better if you have actually done the requisite formulation and presentation of a polished written dissertation product. Then one may luxuriate in the intellectual ambience surrounding a significant, appropriately authored, piece of research.

The Final Oral Meeting. As noted earlier when discussing the Problem Hearing, the usual sequence of events is as follows:

. . . the researcher presents a 10–15 minute overview of the study, the findings and their implications for theory, research and practice in whatever format desired (e.g.; accompanied by slides, etc.);

. . . the advisor, who serves as the convenor, requests input from committee members and a discussion ensues, in which the candidate is expected to non-defensively deliberate about the issues raised;

. . . upon the conclusion of the inquiry, the advisor (often with the candidate outside the room) secures a consensus among committee members as to the status of the dissertation. Usually this involves an acceptance of the dissertation but with some specific changes being required. Then the committee's decision is conveyed to the candidate along with commendation for completing the study in both oral and written form;

. . . if the Committee is ready to sign the Acknowledgement page, signatures are secured. The candidate would be well advised to bring one-half dozen copies of the Approval sheets and black pens;

. . . after the Committee leaves, you and your Advisor decide essentially on the manner and time line for making the final changes proposed.

It is well to remember that at the time of the final orals that (1) you are the expert on your dissertation and (2) everyone wants you to succeed!

Examples of Questions Which Might Be Asked at the Final Orals. Again while just about anything pertaining to your study might usefully be asked at a final orals session, some questions which might be anticipated might include:

. . . Are there other interpretations which might be offered for the results you found?

. . . What were the surprises for you? The disappointments?

. . . What would you do differently if you were to do the study now?

. . . What did you learn about research?

. . . What did you learn about your subject area?

. . . What does your study say to educators and scholars? To professionals in your field of study?

Submission of the Dissertation: A Check-List

So there you are—this really *is* it. The last changes have been made and you are just about to get the "monkey off your back"—which translated means to make the final delivery of this wonderful work to your Committee members and the library.

To assist you in this final task, the following list of items to be double checked is offered, though specifics vary from institution to institution.

1. Is every page of the dissertation numbered correctly?
2. Is your name, in full, on the title page, the abstract, and the microfilm agreement form?* Is the name identical on all three?
3. Does the title meaningfully describe the contents of your dissertation or thesis? Are words substituted for formulas and symbols?
4. Is the title on the abstract and the agreement form the same, word-for-word, as it is on the dissertation?
5. Are all the charts, graphs and other illustrative materials legible in the manuscript? Are they in the correct order and position?
6. Does the abstract adhere to the maximum length? (350 words for Dissertation Abstracts International; 300 words for Research Abstracts and 150 words for Masters Abstracts).

Usually you submit two (2) copies in manilla folders to the appropriate library person and a bound copy (black binders are usually preferred) to *each* committee member with an expression of appreciation for their services. See your own institution's requirements for specific submission and payment of fees procedures. Oh yes, you pay for the privilege of this final procedure (e.g., microfilming costs, binding fees, etc.). and remember, after all the previous efforts and expenditures, this is but a small and final price to pay for the opportunity to share your work with the world of scholars who will seek out your manuscript.

*This is a form furnished by your school. Read the instructions carefully before filling it out.

Chapter Nine
Life After the Dissertation
Eileen T. Nickerson, Ph.D.

The Recovery/Reconstitution Period

Yes, there is life after a dissertation is completed. Frequently, the process of a dissertation requires so much time and energy, that one encounters a feeling of loss of focus and purpose afterwards. It is to be expected that despite the arduous labor, this effort has become an important part of one's existence and identity. Furthermore, a dissertation may allow one to be somewhat neglectful of some aspects of one's personal and professional life. The completion of the dissertation often serves as a signal to others that you and your energies are now freed and available—precisely at the time when you may be feeling let down, tired and unfocussed.

Adding perhaps to your dilemma, your dissertation committee frequently suggests to you that you should professionally present and publish your work. While it is to your professional benefit to follow this advice, you may want to allow yourself some time to recover, reflect and re-invest in your personal relationships and professional work before you return to the task of dissertation dissemination. In doing so, reward yourself for your newly acquired and richly deserved status. If possible, take some time off and reconstitute your energies. Then you may find yourself more ready to tackle those "show-casing" opportunities to present your work in various professional forums including professional publications.

Professional Presentations

All professional organizations offer various opportunities for its members to present and exchange views about their professional endeavors. Usually there are international, national, regional, state-wide and local area meetings. Announcements of these meetings and solicitation of presentation proposals are frequently published in the organizational journals and newsletters. The solicitation usually contains information needed to submit to the professional group. Your dissertation committee members may also be helpful to you in deciding where, when and how to present your work. They may also suggest you join them in some presentation or agree to sponsor your dissertation project offering.

You would be well advised to think of several professional forums and types of professional presentations. For example, you may wish to deliver a paper on the overall thrust of your dissertation to a relevant professional group; while presenting your methodology or set of measures to a professional group specifically oriented to these concerns. And lastly, you may wish to organize a workshop, seminar or symposia around your findings and their implications.

As an example, one such theme of professional presentations was pursued by a group of graduates from our program and myself—the graduates having done their dissertations in the area of understanding and employing strategems for modifying the stereotypic sex role socialization effects with various groups of adolescent females. Besides individual paper presentations, we presented as a symposia under the general rubric of "Addressing Female Adolescent Needs" to a variety of professional organizations including American Association of Counseling and Development, the Eastern Educational Research Association, the Interamerican Congress on Psychology, and the International Association for Applied Psychology.

In the process of presenting, we all gained an opportunity to share our work with interested professionals, to learn of their related work and to expand our network of supportive professional colleagues. It is such an important aspect of one's professional development that I would encourage you to be responsibly assertive and indicate your interest in presenting to your advisor and members of your committee, so that they may alert you to possibilities. You may ask for their suggestions, support and even their presence at your presentation!

Professional Publishing

Unfortunately, much of the energy, enthusiasm and ideas engendered by the dissertation process is often lost to the larger scholarly audience which might usefully have been addressed. Many graduate students who complete dissertations avoid publishing because they don't know how to get properly started, overemphasize the problems involved in publishing, and/or are fearful of having their manuscripts rejected.

Additionally, potential contributors to professional journals have a number of questions surrounding the mechanism of getting published. These include: What are the steps that lead to being published? Of what use are query letters? How long should you wait for a decision for acceptance or rejection? And how can you increase your chances of getting your manuscript published? These queries will be addressed in the paragraphs to follow, though the comments will be primarily directed at publication in professional journals.

Steps to Getting Published. One of the most important steps in publishing one's work is to select the appropriate journal if it is an article or paper, and the appropriate publisher, if its a book. This means getting to know who publishes what. A careful review of recent issues of various journals, for example, will indicate the type of articles typically accepted by each journal. Journal issues also contain informative statements as to the type of article they solicit, where and how to send an article for publication in the journal, etc.

Timing is also considered to be crucial in this selection process. Experienced contributors to journals, for example, keep tabs on journals which publish theme issues and they know which themes are coming up and when. A good article is much less likely to be accepted when a journal has just published a theme issue on the same topic. Book publishers also may be less willing to publish a text which will compete with a recently published work of a similar nature.

Related to timing is the contemporary nature of topic of the article or book. Certain themes are considered more current at various points and are more likely to be the subject of interest, controversy or inquiry.

When actually submitting the article for publication, pay careful attention to the "Guidelines for Publishing" which the publisher provides. It is also considered helpful to have a discerning and knowledgeable colleague read the manuscript critically. Obviously, one needs to proof-read the copy before and after typing and before submission.

It is also suggested that you expect to revise a manuscript which you have submitted, as revisions are requested of the vast majority of manuscripts accepted for publication. Revisions requested may run from a minor touch-up to a major overhaul. Though the requisite alterations may eventually be experienced as helpful, some "cooling-off" period after their receipt may be desireable before you set about responding to them.

The Advisability of a Query Letter. Writers also ask whether they should send query letters before they submit an article. Experienced editors and authors tend to disagree on this question. Henson (1984) found that two-thirds of the forty educational journal editors which he surveyed said they did not want query letters. Of those one-third who did prefer to receive them, they claimed that such letters served the interest of potential contributors. For this reason experienced authors recommend using such letters, as they can save time and energy. For example, if a certain topic is not considered suitable for a given journal, or if the journal has just carried a similar article, the editor can easily inform the would-be-contributor.

Time Lines for Submission and Manuscript Publication. As noted previously, authors-to-be wonder about how long they should wait for a response to a query letter and for the acceptance or rejection of their manuscript. Additional advice given to an aspiring author would include the injunction to be prepared for publication to take some time and effort, just as the initial manuscript preparation did. Typically, while you may expect to receive an acknowledgement of a manuscript's arrival in two to three weeks, editors may take from between three to six months to respond to a manuscript and from between six months to a year between receipt of a manuscript to its publication.

The evaluation of a manuscript usually takes even longer if it is submitted to a refereed journal. Refereed journals mail manuscripts to the referer, wait for their responses and then evaluate the manuscript in light of the (sometimes divergent) responses. Submission of book/text manuscripts likewise usually take longer because of the lengthier review and feedback process.

Increasing Your Chances of Being Published. Every author wants the answers to this one. Henson (1984) in his survey of forty educational journal editors found that almost half of them said that an accompanying photo would increase the chances. The best photos to send are black and white glossy prints; one-third prefer 8×10s, 30% prefer 5×7s and 28% prefer 3×5s.

The editors in Henson's (1984) survey indicated that the most common mistake would-be-contributors make is to fail to acquaint themselves with the journal and its reader. They indicated that prospective authors should read the suggestions to contributors which are published regularly by some journals and made available by mail to others.

The editors also suggested that would-be-authors avoid jargon and write with their readers in mind. They indicated they should use direct and conversational language and they should "spice their manuscripts with concrete examples wherever possible" (Henson, 1984, p. 637). And how do you avoid a hard-to-read and labored style? How do you make your writing easy and interesting to read? The same way you accomplished this feat while writing your dissertation—namely, by rewriting, rewriting and rewriting some more.

Summary and Overview

The journey you have taken to this "life after a dissertation" has been a laborious but significant one, with much personal and professional growth admidst the pain and struggle. So it will be to find a full professional life afterwards. It has been the intention in this chapter to aid you to the fullest possible existence by discussing some aspects of this "life after"—namely, the sharing of your work at professional meetings and through publication in professional journals and texts. The articulation of your work to a larger professional audience is a significant part and dimension of your newly found professional status and it represents the final fruits of your dissertation labors.

Appendix A
Using the Library and Locating Essential Resources*

The library shelves will yield a number of guides to basic reference books and sources. One that reference librarians often turn to:

Sheehy, E. (Ed.). *Guide to Reference Books*. (9th Ed.). Chicago: American Library Association, 1976. A guide to major reference books of all kinds from all over the world. This work is sometimes referred to as the "Winchell", having been edited at one time by Constance Winchell. Like *Dissertations Abstracts International,* the Sheehy guide can yield information on existing theses in a particular subject and can tell you how to locate more information. On any number of topics, Sheehy offers valuable advice and points the scholar in the proper direction.

Downs, R. B. and Keller, C. D. *How to Do Library Research*. Urbana: University of Illinois Press, 1975. Lists hundreds of reference books, including specialized reference books for certain fields or knowledge—from accounting to medicine, from railroads and motor coaches to writing; 133 pages are devoted to specialized subjects alone.

The fast pace of our modern world has the effects of making many books out of date almost before they appear on the library shelves. To keep abreast of current developments, you will need to tap the vast pool of information fed by journals, reports, monographs, newspapers, and other periodicals. The guides to such publications include:

Poole's Index to Periodical Literature: 1801–1881. (3rd ed. rev.) Boston: Houghton Mifflin, 1891. In two volumes. Five supplements covering 1882 to 1906. This is primarily a subject index. Long the best source for the nineteenth-century periodicals, it is beginning to be displaced by *Nineteenth Century Readers' Guide,* which is proceeding backward from 1900. See also M. V. Bell and J. C. Bacon, "Poole's Index": Date & Volume Key . . . Chicago: Association of College and Reference Libraries, 1957.

Reader's Guide to Periodical Literature. New York: Wilson, 1900–Semimonthly with quarterly and annual cumulations; about 130

*Adapted from Madsen, D. (1983). *Successful dissertation and theses.* San Francisco: Jossey-Bass, Inc., 101–106.

popular periodicals are indexed by author and subject. (Before 1929 it covered many education journals now listed in the Education Index.)

A newspaper index can be as perfunctory as a card file; in such you will have to do a little digging to find the information you need. At times like these, you will be grateful for:

Index To The (London) Times. London: The Times, 1906–. Bimonthly.

New York Times Index. New York: New York Times Co., 1913–. If an event has been reported in the New York Times, you may be able to fix the date and then consult the local papers for more extensive news coverage. This index comes out biweekly and is cumulated every year; the classification scheme is broad and detailed.

Other guides to periodicals include:

Biological and Agricultural Index. New York: Wilson, 1964.

Education Index. New York: Wilson, 1929. Over 250 education journals are indexed.

ERIC Educational Documents Index. Washington, D.C.: U.S. Government Printing Office, 1966–. This is an index to the research documents in the Educational Resources Information Center. The local library may be able to give you a copy of ERIC holdings available on microfilm.

Humanities Index. New York: Wilson, 1974–. 260 periodicals are listed by subject and title.

Index to U.S. Government Periodicals. Chicago: Infordot Informational, 1972–. Comes out quarterly, is cumulated every year. One hundred or so government periodicals are indexed, and a computer-printed guide is published.

Social Sciences Index. New York: Wilson, 1974–. Formerly combined with the *Humanities Index* as the *Social Sciences and Humanities Index.* Over 250 periodicals are listed.

To locate a periodical the local library may not have, you can consult the various indexes to international periodicals and the Union List of Serials in Libraries of the United States.

Statistics and Facts

Digest of Education Statistics. Washington, D.C.: U.S. Government Printing Office, 1962–. Contains statistical information on a wide variety of educational matters.

The Fact Book: The American Almanac. New York: Grosset & Dunlap, 1964–. A paperback reprint of the Statistical Abstract of The United States.

Statistical Abstract of The United States. Washington, D.C.: U.S. Government Printing Office, 1879–.

World Almanac—Book of Facts. New York: Newspaper Enterprise Association, 1868–.

Biographic Information

A plethora of biographical information is available, from the detailed biography of a single individual to books that record biographical data on thousands of persons. Most often consulted are:

Biography Index: A Cumulative Index to Biographical Material in Books and Magazines. New York: Wilson, 1946–. A quarterly index by name, profession, or occupation with three-year cumulations.

Cattell, J. (Ed.). *American Men and Women of Science.* (10th Ed.) New York: Bowker, 1906–.

Dictionary of American Biography (21 vols. plus 7 supplements and an index). New York: Scribner's, 1928–1981. Includes only persons no longer living.

Directory of American Scholars. New York: Bowker, 1942–.

Jones, V., and others. *Family History For Fun & Profit.* Salt Lake City: Genealogical Copy Service, 1972.

Notable Names in American History: A Tabulated Register. Clifton, NJ: White, 1973.

Who's Who In America. Chicago: Marquis, 1899–. Published every other year, it contains thousands of names. This company also publishes many other similar books, such as Who's Who In Government.

Who Was Who In America. Chicago: Marquis, 1942–. Published every ten years, it lists prominent persons now deceased.

And, finally, a one-volume work:

Webster's Biographical Dictionary. Springfield, MA: Merriam, 1972. Over 50,000 short biographies, most of them only a few lines in length.

Manuscripts

Archives, manuscripts, and other "primary" source materials are usually housed and organized separately from the other library materials. The best approach is through the curator of manuscripts. It also pays to become familiar with the guides to various state and local historical society collections, as well as:

Hamer, P. M. *A Guide to Archives & Manuscripts in the United States.* New Haven, Conn.: Yale University Press, 1961.

The National Union Catalog of Manuscript Collections. Washington, D.C.: Library of Congress, 1971.

Encyclopedias

The various multivolume encyclopedias, such as *Encyclopedia Britannica,* need no instruction. Others to be considered are:

Dictionary of American History. (Rev. Ed.). New York: Scribner's, 1976.

International Encyclopedia of Higher Education. (9 vols. & index. San Francisco: Jossey-Bass, 1977.

International Encyclopedia of The Social Sciences. (16 vols. & index). New York: Macmillan & Free Press, 1968. A superior example of a specialized authoritative encyclopedia.

The New Columbia Encyclopedia. New York: Columbia University Press, 1975. Single volume.

Computer Based Information Retrieval Systems

Information on social and community interventions is available through a variety of sources including automated information retrieval systems, abstracting and indexing services, government publications, informal reports of research projects, proceedings, dissertations, pamphlets, and specialized publications. A brief list of information sources is cited below:

Search System

Automated search and retrieval systems represent the quickest and most efficient method of bibliographic control. The search system includes:

1. *PsychINFO*—American Psychological Association, 1200 17th Street, N.W., Washington, D.C. 20036, the automated data base version of *Psychological Abstracts.*
2. *Computer Information Services of the National Clearinghouse for Mental Health Information (NCMHI)*—Alcohol, Drug Abuse, and Mental Health Administration, 5600 Fishers Lane, Rockville, MD. 20852. Reader generated bibliographics are available without charge to anyone within the mental health professions.
3. *Data Bank of Program Evaluation (DBPE)*—School of Public Health, U.C.L.A., 10833 LeConte Avenue. Los Angeles, CA. 90024. A computerized field of brief reports of evaluations in the mental health field appearing in over 100 journals and unpublished sources since 1969.
4. *National Technical Information Service (NTIS)*—5285 Port Royal Rd., Springfield, VA 22151. A semi-monthly, computer printed, bibliographic data base by the U.S. Department of Commerce for Information generated under federally funded research. NTIS also issues *Behavior & Society,* a weekly news service.
5. *Lockheed Information Sources*—3251 Hanover Street, Palo Alto, CAL. 94304. A commercial data base including *Psychological Abstracts,* ERIC, and NTIS.

Indexing and Abstracting Services

In addition to *Psychological Abstracts* and the *Catalog of Selected Documents in Psychology,* published by the American Psychological Association, five other helpful indexing and abstracting services for the topic of social and community interventions are:

1. *Social Sciences Citation Index*—Institute for Scientific Information, 325 Chestnut St., Philadelphia, PA. 19106. Issued three times a year. Access to information is also available through a Permuterm (subject) index, corporation index, and source index.

2. *Bulletin of The Public Affairs Information Service* (PAID)—Public Affairs Information Service, Inc., 11 West 40th St., New York, NY 10018. A selective list of latest books, pamphlets, government publications, reports of public and private agencies, periodical articles relating to economic and social conditions, public administration and international relations published in English throughout the world. Issued weekly except for the last two weeks of each quarter.

3. *Subject Guide to Forthcoming Books*—R. R. Bowker Company, 1180 Avenue of the Americas, New York, NY 10036. A list of books expected to be published in the United States during the next five months. Issued bimonthly.

4. *Journal of Human Services/Abstracts*—Project Share, P.O. Box 2309, Rockville, MD 20852. January 1976 was the first issue of this quarterly journal of documents. Project Share makes available a broad range of documentation of subjects of concern to those responsible for the planning, management, and delivery of human service.

5. *Education Resources Information Center* (ERIC)—National Institute of Education, Washington, D.C. 20208. Indexes and abstracts documents processed through clearinghouses in the ERIC system. Contains author, subject, and institution indexes. Issued monthly.

Federal System

The following federal government sources are recommended for the topic of social and community interventions:

1. *Monthly Catalog of United States Government Publications*—Superintendent of Documents, U.S. Government Printing Office, Washington, D.C. 20402.

2. *Index of U.S. Government Periodicals*—Infordata International, Inc., Suite 4602, 175 #. Delaware Place, Chicago, IL., 60611. Published in May, August, November, and March.

3. *CIS/Index to Publications of the U.S. Congress and American Statistics Index*—Published by the Congressional Information Service Inc. 7101 Wisconsin Avenue, Washington, D.C. 20014. A comprehensive guide and

index to the statistical publications of the U.S. government. These two sources will yield valuable data concerning hearings, witnesses, proposals, legislation, and other vital information including corresponding statistical data related to federal government activities in the mental health field.

Specialized Sources

1. *InterDOK*—A directory of published proceedings, InterLOK Corporation, P.O. Box 326, Harrison, NY 10528, is a bibliographic directory of preprints and published proceedings of congresses, conferences, symposia, meetings, seminars, and summer schools. Issued monthly 10 times a year, September to June.
2. *Research Grants Index*—U.S. National Institutes of Health, Division of Research Grants, Bethesda, MD 20014. This annual publication provides information on health research currently being conducted by non-Federal institutions and supported by the health agencies of the Department of Health, Education and Welfare.
3. *Public Affairs Pamphlets*—381 Park Avenue, S., New York, NY 10016, issues interesting and easy-to-read pamphlets addressing problems in mental health, family relations, social problems, etc.
4. *Alternatives in Print: Catalog of Social Change Publications, 1975–76*— A specialized guide to publications available from nonprofit, antiprofit, counterculture, Third World movement groups and the free press.

The personal and informal exchange of information among us still remains one of the most important and most valuable information source.

Appendix B
Foundations and Research Grants

Periodic Guides to Foundations

The Foundation Center Source Book. New York: The Foundation Center
"Documentation on large grant-making foundations—entity descriptions, policies, programs, application procedures, and grants." One hundred listings (of the largest foundations) with in-depth coverage. Arranged alphabetically.

The Foundation Directory. New York: The Foundation Center
Treats foundations with assets of at least one million dollars making grants totaling at least $500,000 per annum. 2,533 listings arranged by state.

Foundations That Send Their Annual Report. New York: Public Service Materials Center
Over four hundred foundations with assets of at least one million dollars making grants totaling at least $200,000 per annum.

The Survey of Grant-Making Foundations With Assets of Over $1 Million or Grants of Over $200,000. New York: Public Service Materials Center
Unique coverage of granting foundations; lists foundations according to whether or not they have a "best time of year" to receive applications, whether or not their grants cover operating expenses, etc.

Where America's Large Foundations Make Their Grants. New York: Public Service Materials Center
Lists grants of at least one thousand dollars; notes total number of grants less than one thousand dollars. 750 entries including (in some cases) the purpose for which the grant was made. Arranged alphabetically.

Greater Boston Foundations. Westwood, MA: J. F. Gray Company
Treats Boston area foundations making grants totaling at least $100,000 per annum. Includes major recipients of the grants.

Periodic Guides to Grants

Directory of Research Grants. Scottsdale, Arizona: Oryx Press
Entries are brief descriptions of grant and grant programs in order by a subject classification system. Includes grants names and sponsoring organizations indexes.

The Grants Register. New York: St. Martin's Press
Subject indexes for citizens and residents of various countries (including

the U.S.). Helpful for exchange opportunities and/or international scholarships and grants.

Guides to Application for Grants

How to Raise Funds from Foundations. New York: Public Service Materials Center.

How to Write Successful Foundation Presentations. New York: Public Service Materials Center.

Academic Media

200 E. Ohio Street
Chicago, IL 60611

Annual Register of Grant Support (CARGS)

More than 2,000 grant support programs are fully identified. Available at Mugar Library, reference desk.

Directory of Scholarly and Research Publication Opportunities

Under one cover, publishing opportunities in the humanities, social sciences and sciences are brought together. Available at reference desk, Mugar Library.

Behavior Today

Del Mar, CA 92014
Money and How to Get It

A comprehensive report culled from *Behavior Today* supplements. It includes procedural advice and reference material on foundations, federal granting agencies and funding sources.

Walton, J. *Writing small grants for graduate students.* Unpublished comprehensive treatise, Boston University, 1975.

White, V. P. *Grants: how to find out about them and what to do next.*

Miscellaneous Information

The Foundation Center (888 Seventh Avenue, New York, New York 10019) maintains files on over 26,000 grant-making foundations in the United States. The Center's Libraries are located in New York and Washington, D.C.

Appendix C
Review of Projects Involving Human Subjects

Information Regarding Informed Consent

By law, any experimental subject or clinical patient who is exposed to possible physical, psychological, or social injury must give informed consent prior to participating in a proposed project. New regulations promulgated by the Department of Health, Education, and Welfare define informed consent as "the knowing consent of an individual or his legally authorized representative so situated as to be able to exercise free power of choice wihout undue inducement or any element of force, fraud, deceit, duress, or other form of constraint or coercion."

In most cases, informed consent is best obtained by having the subject read a document (the Informed Consent Form) presenting all information pertinent to the investigation or project and affixing a signature indicating that they have read the document and giving their consent to participation under the conditions described therein.

On the basis of directives of the Department of Health, Education, and Welfare the project director is requested to include the following items in the Informed Consent Form as appropriate to the project:

1. A general statement of the background of the project and the project objectives.
2. A fair explanation of the procedures to be followed and their purposes, including identification of any procedures which are experimental.
3. A description of any benefits reasonably to be expected and, in the case of treatment, disclosure of any appropriate alternative procedures that might be advantageous for the subject.
4. An offer to answer any queries of the subject concerning procedures or other aspects of the project.
5. An instruction that the subject is free to withdraw consent and to discontinue participation in the project or activity at any time without prejudice to the subject.
6. An instruction that, in the case of the questionnaires and interviews, the subject is free to deny to answer specific items or questions.
7. An instruction that, if services or treatment are involved in the setting or context of the project, neither will they be enhanced nor diminished as a

result of the subject's decision to volunteer or not to volunteer participation in the project.

8. An explanation of the procedures to be taken to insure the confidentiality of the data and information to be derived from the subject.

If the subject is to be videotaped or photographed in any manner, this must be disclosed in the Informed Consent Form. The subject must be told the name of the person who will have custody of such videotapes or photographs, who has access to the videotapes or photographs, how they are to be used, and what will be done with them when the study is completed. When one-way viewing windows are to be employed, the number and composition of the viewing group should be described.

The Informed Consent document must not contain any exculpatory language or any other waiver of legal rights releasing, or appearing to release, the investigator, project director, or the institution from liability.

At the bottom of the Informed Consent Form, provision should be made for the signature of the subject (and date signed) and/or a legally authorized representative. It is generally advisable to precede this with a statement to the effect that the subject and/or representative have read the statement and do understand.

There is also concern about the methods for recruitment of subjects and patients with special attention to situations involving possible pressure or coercion. Full clarification is needed regarding projects which will involve students enrolled in a University course, where financial reimbursement is involved, or the potential subject is an inmate of a custodial or punitive institution. The intent of the request for clarification is the satisfaction of the reviewers that no potential participant feels an obligation to participate or is doing so out of material need.

In the case of minors, one or both parents should sign as appropriate. For minors of sufficient maturity, signatures should be obtained from the subject and the parent(s). State laws usually define minors as persons under 18 years of age.

Appendix D
Critical Evaluation of Sources*

Gathering information for your paper involves critical evaluation of sources for authority and dependability and the use of an accurate, efficient system for taking notes.

As you select works to read and sources to use in your paper, you should continually evaluate the materials with regard to the primary or secondary nature of each source, its objectivity, qualifications of the author, and the level of each source (its intended audience).

Primary and Secondary Sources. You should consider whether a particular source is a primary or secondary work for your purposes. Primary works are basic materials with little or no annotation or editing, such as manuscripts, diaries, letters, interviews, and laboratory reports. Secondary materials derive from primary materials and include analysis, interpretation, and commentary on primary materials. Depending on the point of view of the research paper, the same materials may be considered either primary or secondary. A research paper on the contribution of E. B. White, a writer and editor, to *The New Yorker* magazine would treat White's articles in the magazine as primary materials. It would treat as a secondary source Brendan Gill's *Here at the New Yorker,* an account of the editorial leadership of the magazine during the years White worked there. The writer of a paper on Brendan Gill, however, would considered *Here at the New Yorker* a primary source. Your topic may require an emphasis on either primary or secondary sources or a combination of the two.

Objectivity. The objectivity of a source is its lack of bias or prejudice. Total objectivity is not humanly possible, but the most valuable sources identify any biases that might be caused by the author's affiliations or allegiances—whether economic, political, philosophical, or religious—and any limitations inherent in the author's approach or the materials used. A writer with investments in farms producing soybeans, for example, should indicate the possibility of bias for economic reasons in a study on the relative advantages of soybeans and seaweed as bases for new foods. Similarly, the writer of a study of the automotive industry based on information obtained from executives at Chrysler or

*Adapted from Campbell, W. G., Ballou, S. V., and Slade, C. (1982). *Form and style: theses, reports, term papers.* 6th Ed. Boston: Houghton Mifflin Company.

Ford should make readers aware that the nature of the sources may influence his or her conclusions in certain ways. Even if the writer does not reveal possible reasons for bias, you should be aware of the writer's point of view and evaluate the work accordingly.

Qualifications of the Author. The qualifications of the author that might influence your choice of a source include academic degrees, professional credentials, work experience, and status in the field. This kind of information may be found in preliminary or appendix materials in the source itself, in a biographical dictionary or directory such as WHO'S WHO, or in an encyclopedia. The information may indicate the quality, nature, and objectivity of a source.

Level. The intended audience for a work determines its level in areas such as diction, sentence structure, complexity, and assumed background knowledge. Particularly if you are an undergraduate, you may find some sources too technical and advanced, and you should either seek guidance in understanding them or omit them.

References

American Chemical Society (1978). *Handbook for authors of papers in American Chemical Society Publications*. Washington, D.C.'s American Chemical Society.

American Institute of Biological Sciences (1972). *CBE style manual* (3rd ed.). Washington, D.C.: American Institute of Biological Sciences.

American Medical Association (1966). *Style book and editorial manual* (4th ed.). Chicago: American Medical Association.

American Psychological Association (1982). *Ethical principles in the conduct of research with human participants*. Washington, D.C.: American Psychological Association.

American Psychological Association (1983). *Publications Manual of the American Psychological Association* (3rd ed.). Washington, D.C.: American Psychological Association.

American Psychological Association (1975). Special Issue: Instrumentation in psychology. *American Psychologist, 30*(3).

American Psychological Association (1976). Task Force on Health Research. Contribution of psychology to health. *American Psychologist, 31*(4), 263–274.

Ary, D., Jacobs, L. C., and Razavich, A. (1979). *Introduction to research in education* (2nd ed.). NY: Holt, Rinehart & Winston.

Barlow, D. H., Hayes, S. C. & Nelson, R. O. (1985). *The scientist practitioner: Research and accountability in clinical and educational settings*. Elmsford, NY: Pergamon Press, Inc.

Barlow, D. H. & Hersen, M. (1984). *Single case experimental designs: Strategies for studying behavior change*. (2nd ed.). Elmsford, NY: Pergamon Press.

Bellack, A. S. & Hersen, M. (1985). *Research methods in clinical psychology*. Elmsford, NY: Pergamon Press.

Campbell, D. T. & Stanley, J. C. (1963). *Experimental and quasi-experimental designs for research*. Chicago: Rand McNally.

Campbell, W. G., Ballou, S. V. & Slade, C. (1982). *Form and style: Theses, reports, term papers*. (6th ed.). Boston: Houghton Mifflin.

Cronbach, L. J. (1980). *Toward a reform of program evaluation*. San Francisco: Jossey-Bass.

Davidson, D. (1977). *Theses and dissertations: An information source*. Hamden, CT: Linnet Books.

Davis, G. B. & Parker, C. (1979). *Writing the doctoral dissertation: A systematic approach*. Woodbury, NY: Barron's Educational Service, 1979.

Davitz, J. R. & Davitz, L. L. (1978). *Evaluating research proposals in the behavioral sciences.* NY: Teachers College Press.

Directory of publishing opportunities (1979). Chicago: Marquis Academic Media.

Dixon, W. J. (ed.) (1975). *BMDP: Biomedical computer programs.* Los Angeles: University of California Press.

Downs, R. B. & Keller, C. (1975). *How to do library research.* Urbana: University of Illinois Press.

Drew, C. J. (1985). *Designing and conducting behavioral research.* Elmsford Park, NY: Pergamon Press.

Forward, J., Canter, R. & Kirsch, N. (1976). Role enactment and deception methodologies: alternative paradigm? *American Psychologist, 31*(8), 595–604.

Francis, J. B., Bork, C. E. & Carstens, S. P. (1979). *The proposal cookbook.* Action Research Associates.

Gardner, D. G. & Beatty, J. G. (1980). *Dissertation proposal guidebook.* Springfield, Ill: Chas. C. Thomas.

Harmon, L. R. (1978). *A century of doctorates: Data analysis of growth and change.* Washington, D.C.: National Academy of Sciences.

Harri, R. & Lamb, R. (1981). *The encyclopedia dictionary of psychology.* Cambridge, MA: MIT Press.

Henson, K. T. (1984). Writing for professional publication. Ways to increase your success. *Phi Delta Kappa,* May, 635–637.

Hogan, R., DeSoto, C. B. & Solano, C. (1977). Traits, tests and personality research. *American Psychologist, 32*(4), 255–264.

Holmes, O. (1976). Thesis to Book: What to do with what is left. In E. Harman & I. Montagnes (Eds.). *The thesis and the book.* Toronto: U. of Toronto Press.

Johnson, N. (1982). Publishing: how to get started. *Personnel & Guidance Journal,* 321–323.

Jordan, L. (Ed.) (1982). *The New York Times manual of style & usage,* (2nd ed.). New York: Times Books.

Kerlinger, F. N. (1979). *Behavioral research: A conceptual approach.* New York: Holt, Rinehart & Winston.

Kleeha, W. R., Nie, N. H. & Hull, C. H. (1975). *SPSS Primer.* NY: McGraw Hill.

Kratwohl, D. R. (1977). *How to prepare a research proposal.* Syracuse, NY: University Bookstore.

Lambert, M. J., Christensen, E. R. & DeJulie, S. S. (1982). *The assessment of psychotherapy outcome.* NY: Wiley-Interscience.

Lansbury, P. T. (1975). Selection of thesis research: the most important course. *J. of Chemical Education,* 52–510–511.

Leedy, P. D. (1981). *How to read research and understand it.* NY: Macmillan.

_____(1980). *Practical research: Planning & design,* (2nd ed.). NY: Macmillan.

Madsen, D. (1983). *Successful dissertations and theses.* San Francisco, CA: Jossey-Bass Publishers.

Martin, R. (1980). *Writing and defending a thesis or dissertation in psychology and education.* Springfield, Ill.: Chas. C. Thomas.

Modern Language Association (1977). *Modern Language Association (MLA) handbook for writers of research papers, theses and dissertations.* Modern Language Association.

Mosher, R. L. (1974). Knowledge from practice: Clinical research and development in education. *The Counseling Psychologist,* Sept., 73–81.

Mullins, C. J. (1977). *A guide to writing and publishing in the social and behavioral sciences.* Malabar, FL: Robert E. Krieger Publishing Company.

Nickerson, E. T. & Robertson, L. W. (1978). *A dissertation preparation handbook.* Boston: Boston University School of Education.

Norusis, M. J. (1982). *SPSS introductory guide: basic statistics and operations.* NY: McGraw-Hill.

Reid, W. M. (1978). Will the future generations of biologists write a dissertation? *Bioscience, 28,* 651–654.

Roget's (1977). *International Thesaurus* (4th ed.). NY: Crowell.

_____(1965). *Thesaurus of English words and phrases.* NY: St. Martin's.

Rosenthal, R. (1975). *The volunteer subject.* NY: Wiley—Interscience.

Ross-Larson, B. (1982). *Edit yourself: A manual for everyone who works with words.* New York: W. W. Norton.

Simonton, D. K. (1977). Cross sectional time-service experiments: Some suggested statistical analysis. *Psychological Bulletin, 84*(3), 489–502.

Smith, N. A. P. (1977). *Preparing and submitting your doctoral dissertation.* Ann Arbor: Graduate School, University of Michigan.

Spriestersbach, D. C. & Henry, L. D. (1978). The Ph.D. Dissertation: Servant or master? *Improvement of college and university teaching,* Winter, 52–60.

Strunk, W. Jr., & White, E. B. (1979). *The elements of style,* (3rd ed.). NY: Macmillan Publishing Company.

The Counseling Psychologist (1979). Research in Counseling Psychology, *8* (3).

_____(1982). Research in Counseling Psychology II, *10* (4).

The Personnel & Guidance Journal (1981). Special Issue: Bridging the gap between research & practice. (April)

_____(1981). Special Issue: The counselor and research. Part I (May).

_____(1981). Special Issue: The counselor and research. Part II (June).

Tuckman, B. W. (1979). *Evaluating instructional programs.* Boston: Allyn & Bacon.

Turabian, K. (1973). *A manual for writers of term papers, theses and dissertations.* (4th ed.). Chicago: Rand McNally.

University of Chicago Press (1982). *The Chicago manual of style.* (13th ed.). University of Chicago Press.

Webster's (1979) *Seventh new collegiate dictionary.* Springfield, MA: Merriam.

Zinsser, W. (1980). *On writing well* (2nd ed.). NY: Harper & Bros.